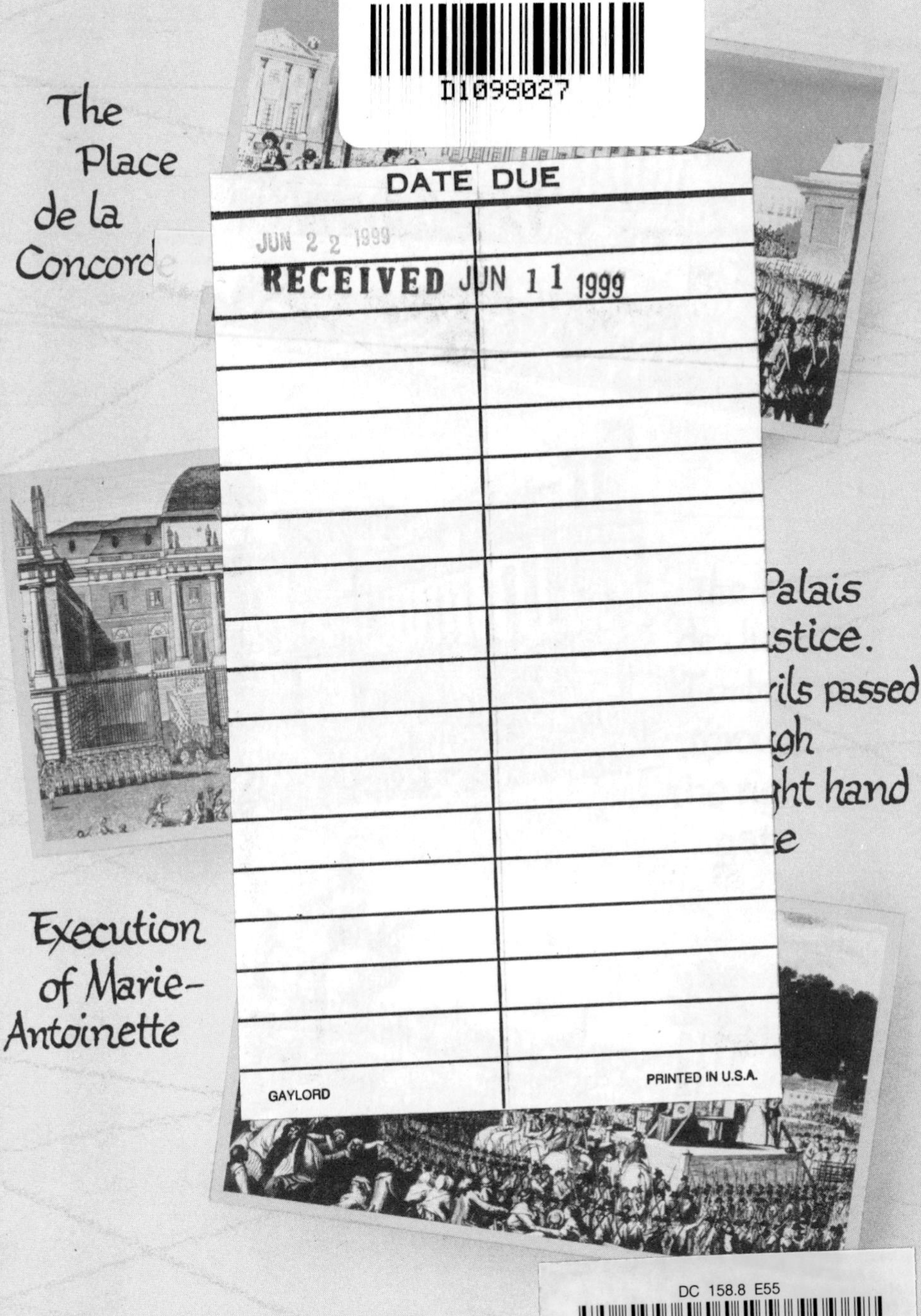

against backgrounds still on vi

THE WAY OF THE TUMBRILS

THE WAY OF THE

TUMBRILS

BY JOHN ELLIOT

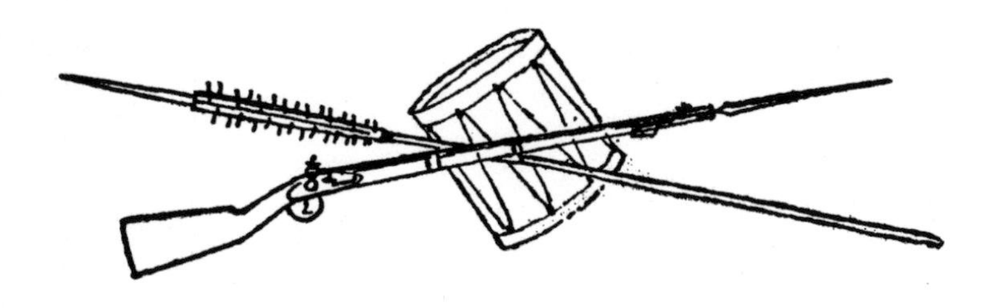

With Illustrations by Peter Roberson

REYNAL & COMPANY NEW YORK

Published by Reynal & Company, Inc.

Library of Congress catalog card number: 58-8136

Printed in the U.S.A. by
American Book–Stratford Press, Inc., New York

To J. B. Morton,
who persuaded me to try, and showed me the way.

ACKNOWLEDGMENTS

My grateful thanks are due to many friends for advice and encouragement during the years it has taken me to collect the material for this book and to write it. I owe a special debt to the following:

M. François Boucher, formerly Director of the Carnavalet Museum, Paris, and M. le Comte Jean de la Monneraye, formerly Director of the Historical Library of the City of Paris, who have given me generously of their expert knowledge;

M. Louis Armand, Chairman of the Board of the French National Railways, for the magnificent gift of a set of contemporary Minutes of the Revolutionary Tribunal, including the record of evidence at the trials of Danton and Marie-Antoinette;

M. Georges Ricroch, Chairman of the Board of the Public Transport Company of Paris, and Mme. Ricroch, for books and photographs of the city;

Mr. P. C. Durrant, formerly Agent-General in France of the British Railways, who made all my appointments and arrangements for me;

Mr. Charles Ede, by whose permission part of the Temple chapter is reproduced from an issue of the Folio Society Magazine; Mr. Peter Green and Mr. Michael Robbins, who read the manuscript with practised eye and kindly admonition; to Miss Elizabeth McIvor, who brought order out of the chaos of paper accumulated over the years; and finally to my wife, who has walked many long and exhausting miles with me, which to her was not always the most attractive way to spend a day in Paris.

To these and many more, too numerous to mention by name, and particularly the kindly people in all parts of Paris to whom I was completely unknown and who, without any introduction, invited me into their homes, gardens and offices, I offer my thanks. Without their help this book must have remained in my head instead of on paper.

J.E.

CONTENTS

FOREWORD

All my life I have been indulging a restless interest in the French Revolution by trying, in my spare time, to catch its echoes among the sights and sounds of modern Paris. A shoe worn by Marie-Antoinette in the Temple Prison and now in a glass case at the Carnavalet Museum; Danton's shaving bowl; the table on which Robespierre lay in agony during his last night with his jaw shattered, waiting for the guillotine; the street where Marat lived and Charlotte Corday found and killed him; the exact place where the tumbrils stood to take on their daily load of victims; the last resting place of the King and Queen; the hall of the terrible Revolutionary Tribunal—these are some of the things I have searched for. It has been an exciting and rewarding labour, and a fascinating way to learn history.

"Excuse me, monsieur; could you tell me, please, if this is where Robespierre lived?"

"Could you point out to me the exact spot where the guillotine was erected for the execution of the King?"

"Does the room still exist in which Louis XVI said

farewell to Marie-Antoinette and his children the night before he died?"

Few events in history have been better or more thoroughly described and analysed than the French Revolution, and in setting down the details of what I have found I am aware that they make no new or serious contribution to our knowledge of it. Nor do they pretend to. Part-time groping for history is most unlikely to add anything to the classic works of Michelet, Aulard and Thiers, the fascinating researches of Lenôtre, the rolling prose of Belloc, the conjured imagery of Carlyle or the brilliant scholarship of J. M. Thompson, Gaetano Salvemini and J. B. Morton, to name a few.

I have made these expeditions into the past against the background of the present because in a latter-day world shaken with revolutions it is still the French Revolution which gives the pattern; its men and women are still the authentic, for-ever-to-be-remembered revolutionaries, its story is still the most romantic and the most terrible. Who would give a Danton for a Trotsky, a Robespierre for a Beria? Is there in history a queen so pinned in tragedy as Marie-Antoinette (except perhaps Mary, Queen of Scots, and here was no revolution)? Only Rasputin, of all the gloomy shadows of the Russian holocaust, seems to have for us something of the same breathless horror. And only something, at that.

There is still nothing in modern history to compare with the pitiless speed and prolonged sweep of the Terror; the drawn-out haunting fate of the little family of King, Queen and children in the Temple; the blinding fanaticism of Charlotte Corday's assassination of Marat in his hip-bath; while of all the instruments of death invented by man, none has the same dreadful fascination as the guillotine.

In fixing the topography of the Revolution as accurately as possible in a greatly changed city, I have tried at the same time to make the drama come alive, to evoke the men and women and the sights and sounds of Paris during the Revolution. Lenôtre wrote his famous *Paris Révolutionnaire* (Perrin) in 1894, and less than twenty years earlier a number of the small streets south of the River which saw so much of the struggle were still in existence. They have long since disappeared. The book was published in English by H. Noel Williams (Hutchinson) in 1925 and is still the classic of its kind. There are of course many guide-books of the period in French, of which two of the most useful are: *Guide Pratique à Travers le Vieux Paris* by the Marquis de Rochegude and Maurice Dumolin (Librairie Edouard Champion), and *Les Pavés de Paris* by Guy de la Batut (Editions Sociales Internationales).

All my notes have been made on the site, and much of the manuscript written in Paris the same night while memory was fresh. Over the years I have revisited the sites and altered the text where the town planner or house builder has made it necessary. Paris continues to alter, however, and it may be that here and there changes have taken place since the book was finished.

I have chosen some of the best known and most easily followed stories of the struggle, in the houses and streets in which they took place. I have read letters and papers, examined doors and walls, climbed dark stairs, looked through ancient windows and stood in the streets outside old houses where great events took place and famous men and women lived and died. Where the buildings remain to this day I have described them as they were during the Revolution, and as they are now. Where they have disappeared and others have risen on their sites, I have written of these, and of the people who now live and work in them. The contrast is often startling, odd, or just amusing, but the past still breaks through.

I have stood on the Pont Neuf at the end of a day tracing out the way of the tumbrils, watching the sun setting on the roofs and spires between the Pont Royal and the Conciergerie, as thousands of men and women saw it setting for the last time, the carts bumping beneath them and the shouts of the mob in their ears; spent many hours in the Place de la Concorde establishing the various emplacements of the guillotine and recapturing, from its noble buildings, the atmosphere of Paris under the Terror, when the executioners worked by day and the grave-diggers of the Madeleine near-by sweated by night; I have wandered in the gardens of the Palais-Royal looking for (and finding) the shop where Charlotte Corday bought the knife that killed Marat, and sat down to rest under the trees where Camille Desmoulins, gesticulating on a table, had set the people alight, so that within two days the Bastille itself had fallen before their fury.

My searches have taken me into dungeons, private houses, public museums, a bakery, and a Catholic seminary, as well as churches, back streets, gardens and doorways all over Paris.

Like Charlotte Corday, we too have a right to be curious, not only about things to come in a troubled world, but about things past, which by their brutal impact on the minds of men brought forth an irresistible challenge to accepted thought, and through cruelties and heroisms alike urged onward man's endless struggle for the rights of man.

JOHN ELLIOT

Paris, August, 1957

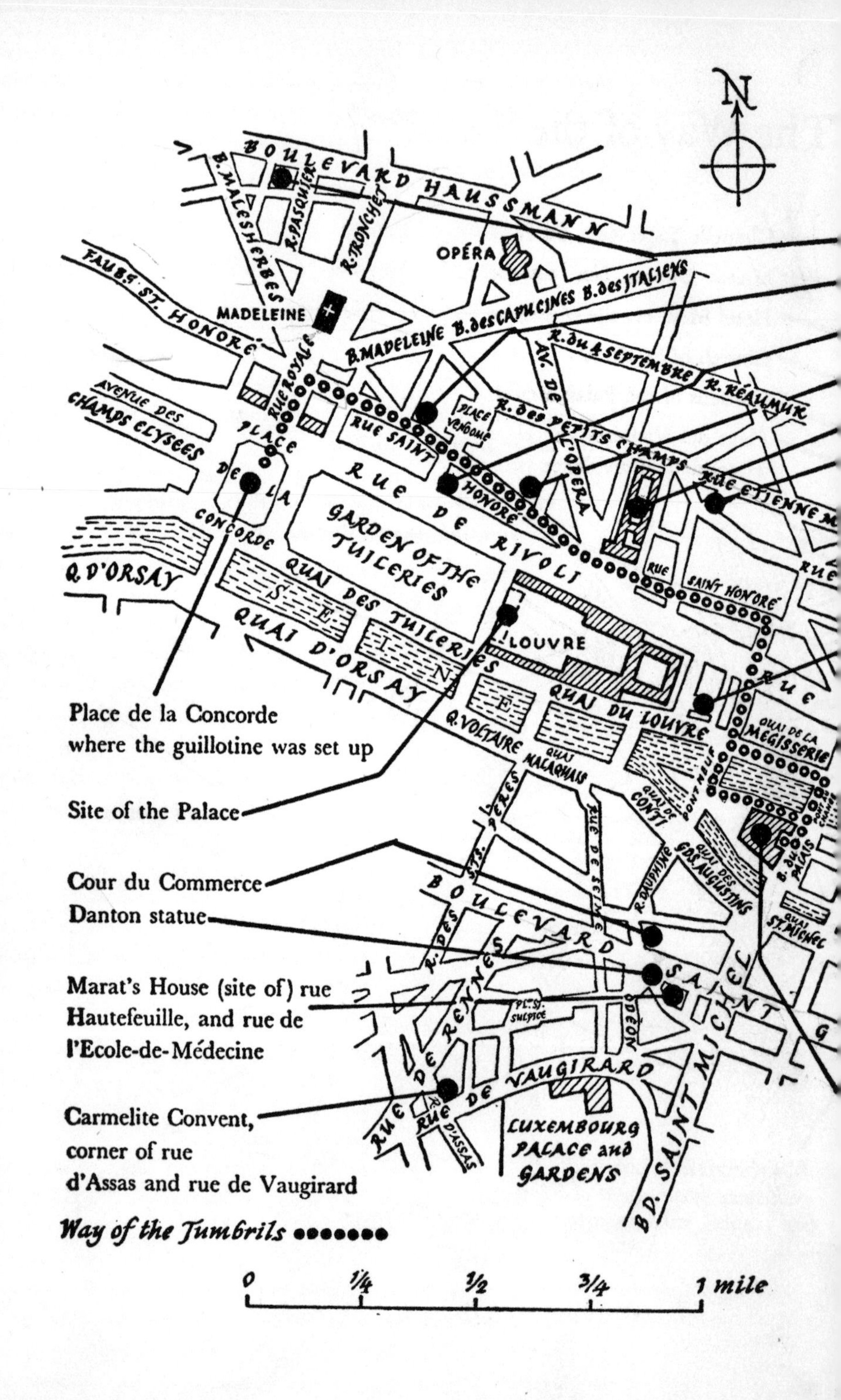
N
BOULEVARD HAUSSMANN
B. MALESHERBES
R. PASQUIER
R. TRONCHET
OPÉRA
FAUBG ST. HONORÉ
MADELEINE
B. MADELEINE
B. des CAPUCINES
B. des ITALIENS
R. du 4 SEPTEMBRE
R. RÉAUMUR
AV. DE L'OPÉRA
RUE ROYALE
AVENUE DES CHAMPS ELYSEES
PLACE VENDOME
R. des PETITS CHAMPS
RUE SAINT HONORÉ
PLACE DE LA CONCORDE
RUE DE RIVOLI
RUE ETIENNE M
GARDEN OF THE TUILERIES
Q. D'ORSAY
QUAI DES TUILERIES
SEINE
QUAI D'ORSAY
RUE SAINT HONORÉ
LOUVRE
QUAI DU LOUVRE
RUE
Q. VOLTAIRE
QUAI MALAQUAIS
QUAI DE LA MEGISSERIE
QUAI DE CONTI
PONT NEUF
RUE DE SEINE
R. DES STS. PÈRES
R. DAUPHINE
QUAI DES GDS. AUGUSTINS
B. DU PALAIS
QUAI ST. MICHEL
BOULEVARD SAINT G
R. DES RENNES
PL. ST. SULPICE
ODÉON
RUE DE VAUGIRARD
RUE DE RENNES
R. D'ASSAS
LUXEMBOURG PALACE and GARDENS
BD. SAINT MICHEL
Place de la Concorde where the guillotine was set up
Site of the Palace
Cour du Commerce
Danton statue
Marat's House (site of) rue Hautefeuille, and rue de l'Ecole-de-Médecine
Carmelite Convent, corner of rue d'Assas and rue de Vaugirard
Way of the Tumbrils
0
1/4
1/2
3/4
1 mile

The Way of the Tumbrils

Chapelle Expiatoire, Bd Haussmann and rue Pasquier

Maison Duplay, Nos. 398-400 rue St Honoré

Hotel Meurice; site of Riding School (Parliament)

Church of St Roch

Gardens of the Palais-Royal

Place des Victoires, rue Hérold (former rue des Vieux Augustins), Hotel de la Providence (site of)

Café de la Parnasse (site of), rue des Prêtres-St Germain l'Auxerrois

National Archives, 60 rue des Francs-Bourgeois

Carnavalet Museum, 23 rue de Sévigné

The Bastille

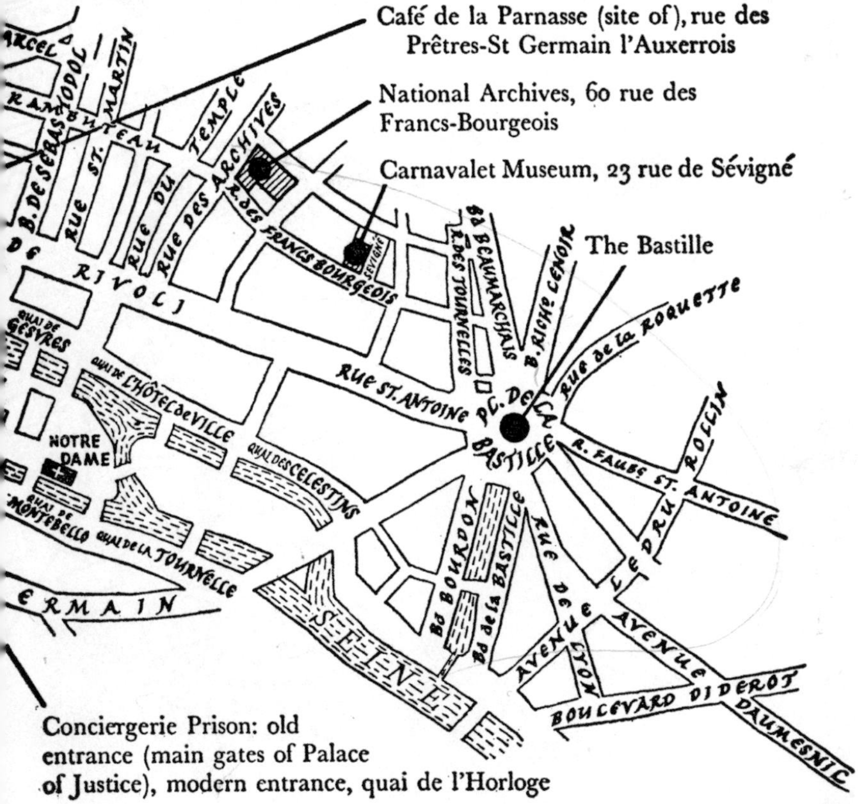

Conciergerie Prison: old entrance (main gates of Palace of Justice), modern entrance, quai de l'Horloge

1. OUTLINE OF THE REVOLUTION

A hundred years before Waterloo there died in Versailles *Le Roi Soleil*—the Sun King, Louis the Fourteenth of France. He was an old man who had once been honoured and feared and now was hated for the immense sums he had spent on wars which the French people paid for in blood and taxation. He left behind great monuments, such as Versailles and the Invalides, a military tradition and glory which were to endure till Napoleon was overthrown, and a bankrupt country sick to death of royal wars and extravagances.

Louis XV, who followed him, had most of his failings and none of his greatness. During his flabby reign, France lost India and Canada to the British, suffering classic defeats at Dettingen, Plassey and Quebec, and endured even harsher taxation than before. King and Court sank into debauchery, while affairs of State were alternately mismanaged by helpless Ministers and irresponsible favourites, of whom Mme. La Pompadour at least had taste and wit, the du Barry her looks. The Court and the armies cost the people millions, and small fortunes were often spent on a single night's banqueting. Meanwhile chaos or starvation was the lot of millions, but not of the *Seigneurs* and their friends. Unrest grew all over France. When in 1774 Louis XV died muttering his "*apres moi, le deluge*," they hurried his diseased body to the grave without farewell or ceremony, and there reigned in his place yet another Louis, the Sixteenth, with Marie-Antoinette of Austria as his Queen.

Louis XVI was twenty years old, and because he was known to be simple, virtuous, and good-natured, and the Queen young and beautiful, the French people, miserable though they were, still clung to the hope of salvation through their sovereign. There was rejoicing everywhere, and men drank the new King's health meaning it.

But the condition of the country after two such reigns called for more than goodwill, and it was not long before the new King was in difficulties. He knew that great reforms were essential, he wanted to bring them about, but he was weak, inconsistent, and worst of all, could never make up his mind. Had he been blessed with only average common sense allied to his native goodness, he might have saved his throne, and France with it, for the idea of a Republic was not seriously considered until the people, desperate and afraid, realised with dismay that Louis had betrayed them; and that was towards the end of the Revolution. Twice at least he had the leading part, and twice at least he would not or could not play it. The tragedy had to run its disordered length, through scenes of suspense and horror to its final hour of dignity on the scaffold. Never did a King make more mistakes in so short a time, and mostly with such good intentions.

The American War of Independence against England in 1775 distracted and puzzled him. He wanted to be neutral, but failed to prevent Lafayette from sailing to help Washington. Thus he embittered relations with the British at a time when he needed friends outside France desperately.

Turgot, one of the first of his Ministers to understand the spirit of the times, tried to alter the basis of taxation in favour of the people, only to be baulked by the stupidity of the nobles and the clergy whom Louis dared not oppose. Necker followed him with schemes for vast loans to re-adjust the national finances. He too failed, and the majority of the *Seigneurs*, as obstinate as they were stupid, reasserted their rights more firmly against the people and even secured the expulsion from the Army of every officer not of noble blood.

By 1789 the tide was too strong to be denied, and the King agreed to call together the old "States-General," which had not sat since 1614. It met at Versailles on May 5. This was Louis' first chance. The new body was elected by universal suffrage, and had he shown some leadership and understanding of the situation he might have led the Revolution himself, for the issue then was not "King versus People" but "People versus Privilege". These men from all over France—ninety per cent of them at least —were still loyal to him as King and looked to him with confidence to show the way to a better life for the people.

Louis could not rise to it; indeed he failed to solve the first real problem—should the States-General sit and vote as one body, or should nobles, clergy and the people—the "Third Estate"—be segregated and vote separately on a basis favourable to the privileged few? After much confused thought, Louis tried to compromise, and when the Third Estate, exasperated, decided to sit on their own as a National Assembly and take control of taxation, the King, pressed by the nobles, ordered their closure. Whereupon the delegates swarmed into the indoor tennis court at Versailles and proclaimed their immortal Rights of Man.

Here was the crucial moment. This was open revolt, and the King had either to support it or suppress it. Characteristically he did neither, still hoping for the best, and when on July 14 the bread-starved Parisians, whipped up by agitators, stormed and captured the Bastille, his first great opportunity had gone. All over France the peasants attacked the castles and chateaux, robbing, burning and slaying in a frenzy of hate and fear.

In Versailles Louis watched and waited, on one hand urged to ratify the Assembly's new Constitution by those who saw the writing on the wall, while on the other the nobles and the clergy, frantic with anger and apprehension, bade him use force at once to crush the revolt before it was too late.

Still Louis clung to his stolid indecision, and the gap was widening rapidly when, on October 5, a mob of Parisian women marched overnight to Versailles, camped in the Palace courtyard and demanded to see the King, swearing they would take him and his family to Paris, and they had their way.

The next day, after a night of bloodshed, the triumphant Parisians led a strange royal procession out of Versailles and on to the road to the capital.

Some hours later, as the royal cavalcade entered the ratridden, overcrowded Palace of the Tuileries, Louis gravely announced that he was happy to come among his people. Neither he, his Queen nor his son were to see Versailles again, or to know more of freedom and hapiness as men know these things, save for a few brief weeks at Saint-Cloud the following summer.

In Catherine de Medici's old Palace, from which hundreds of hangers-on had to be evicted to make room for them, the Royal Family made their uneasy home, while in the Assembly the disciples of Rousseau argued endlessly over the shape of the new State, at the head of which all except a few extremists still wished to see a King. It was to be based on Liberty, Equality, and Fraternity, the Sovereign People were to hold power through their elected delegates, and all would be well.

Behind the doors of the Tuileries other ideas were hatching. Emboldened by the inexperience and confusion of the Assembly, the Queen took heart, and under her influence there grew slowly a plan by which her brother Leopold of Austria, with the Prussians to help him, was to invade France, chastise the people, and restore the Bourbon family to its rightful authority. Only Mirabeau, now near his end, tried to point out the road of safety and wisdom to the King, but Marie-Antoinette, who had always hated Mirabeau, urged Louis on to treachery, and when the great orator and writer died in 1791 there was no one to advise Louis but the Queen.

Thus it was that in June of that year, under the skilled and devoted guidance of the young Count Axel Fersen of Sweden, an admirer of the Queen's at Versailles, the whole family escaped from the Tuileries by night and made for Verdun, where troops were waiting to escort them out of France. How nearly they succeeded, how desperately they failed, how fanatical revolutionaries along the route pierced their disguise and finally halted them near the frontier at Varennes, is one of the great dramas of the Revolution. After an agony of suspense they were brought back to Paris, surrounded every mile of the way by drunken men and women, insulted and jeered at, till in the heat of a blazing June day their lumbering *berline* re-entered a silent Paris and the courtyard of the Tuileries, and the gates closed behind them once more.

By his flight Louis threw away his last hope. Now he was trusted by no one, and the police had found evidence enough when they searched the Palace to make his treason clear. He was forced to accept the new Constitution, which he did with ill-humour, and in April 1792, helpless, he had to declare war against his friends in Austria and Prussia, on the demand of a people blazing with anger at the impertinence of foreign kings who published manifestoes ordering them to free and restore Louis and his family or take the consequence.

The war went badly for France. The Girondins, the middle class liberal revolutionaries in power, were in serious disagreement with the more violent men of the people led by Robespierre and Danton and inflamed by the writings of Marat and Camille Desmoulins. As the bad news streamed in from the fronts, as plan after plan failed, the cry went up that the King and Queen were in touch with the enemy and betraying the country. The massacres in the prisons on September 2, when over two thousand men and women were butchered in a few hours, showed what the nervousness of the government and the temper of the people could permit in the capital city of France.

On August 10 the mobs of Paris attacked the Tuileries, and after a murderous artillery salvo broke into the Palace, killing the Swiss Royal Guards who fought to the last in defence of their master. When most of them were dead or dying, Louis, ineffective as ever, issued his pathetic order for them to cease fire. [You can read the actual message hurriedly written on a piece of paper, in the Carnavalet Museum.] Their heroism had forestalled him. Amid scenes of butchery the Royal Family escaped to the sanctuary of the Riding School nearby, in which the Assembly, soon to be known as the Convention, was sitting in frightened session. Here they stayed, prisoners in a small anteroom for three terrible days, and when at last they were removed to the Temple prison under guard, Louis XVI had been suspended from all his functions, and royalty as such existed in France no more.

On September 21 Dumouriez won the battle of Valmy, the Duke of Brunswick and his Prussians recoiled, and the last hope of the King faded away towards the frontier. He was tried in person by the Convention, and on January 21, 1793, after a heartrending farewell with his family, he was taken in a closed carriage to the Place de la Révolution and there guillotined. He died bravely, in the Catholic faith in which he had been raised, blaming no one and praying for the welfare of the people.

Marie-Antoinette, thin and desperate from weeks of solitary imprisonment, was sent to the Conciergerie Prison in August, and after a trial borne with superb dignity before the Revolutionary Tribunal she went to the scaffold on October 16, in an open cart, her hair grey and her face set like stone. She died to the joy of a people who had hated her for years and believed her to be the main cause of their sorrows.

The King and Queen were followed by all the men who had ruined them. First, in October 1793, fell the men of the Gironde—Vergniaud, Barbaroux, Brissot, Buzot, Madame Roland and all the bright thinkers and talkers, overwhelmed by a crisis which their own speeches had helped to bring about, but which their cultivated minds could not control.

Earlier, in July of that year, Charlotte Corday, the young and saintly philosopher from Caen, had perished as she wished after her assassination of Marat—one of the strangest dramas of history.

As the war fared worse, the Terror grew. Fearful reprisals were taken against royalists and suspects in Paris and the great provincial cities, until, with the French victory at Wattignies in October, Danton and the poet Desmoulins, sickened by the sight and sound of the guillotine, demanded a halt.

For six months the grim struggle went on between Robespierre and Danton, in the Convention, in the revolutionary clubs, and in the Government Committees, until on April 5, 1794, the great orator of the people, the man of action and violence and laughter, passed under the knife he had done so much to sharpen.

Robespierre and St. Just were now alone, but they had not long to live. The incorruptible, now a fanatic, his sense of proportion gone and his judgment warped, let loose a terror such as even Paris had not yet known. Under the frightful "Law of Prairial" (June 1794) men and women could be arrested, tried, and executed without witnesses being called, and the Public Prosecutor, Fouquier-Tinville, saw to it that none escaped whom Robespierre wished to die. The massacre was unending, 1,351 heads falling in one month in Paris alone.

The victory of Jourdan and Klèber at Fleurus in June, which finally freed France from the enemy, made it plain that the need for this deluge of blood was gone. Opposition hardened against Robespierre, and finally he and his younger brother, with St. Just and the crippled Couthon, were arrested after a wild battle of words in the Convention. They were immediately rescued by their friends, but early next morning, the famous Tenth of Thermidor (July 27) they were surprised and re-arrested in the Hotel de Ville. Robespierre was shot in the face, his left jaw broken, and he was carried, lying in agony on a plank, to a table in the Convention and later to the scaffold. He died with his friends as the sun was setting, and a great sigh of relief went up from Paris and all France.

On October 4 of the the following year a crowd of discontented men from the Sections and a number of Royalists attempting a *coup d'etat* converged on the Tuileries Palace to overthrow the Government. The main body was met at the Church of St. Roch in the rue St.

Honoré by salvos from the guns of a young artillery officer, and after many of the rebels had been killed and wounded, his "whiff of grapeshot" gained the day.

The officer's name was Napoleon Bonaparte; the Revolution was over.

Marie-Antoinette

2. MONSIEUR KROK MAKES A BOW

Any study of the Revolution must start at Versailles, the centre of everything in France until the Revolution. Here the French kings (or their mistresses) of two reigns had ruled and misruled, and here the young Louis XVI, fuddled with anxiety at the uproar breaking loose all around him, in 1789 had fatally decided that the people's representatives in his newly-summoned States-General should not sit with the nobles, and when they refused to accept his decision, had ordered their assembly to be closed. Thus did one of the mildest kings in history set fire to his world, and himself perish in the conflagration.

It was in a tennis court, the famous *Jeu de Paume*, that the indignant and frustrated delegates had locked themselves and taken their binding oath never to separate alive until the dignity and freedom of mankind had been secured in a new and liberal constitution. Here, in Versailles, revolution blazed up, and it is in the *Jeu de Paume* first that we may breathe its fiery blast.

From outside it is not an imposing place, and you have to go down a side street to find it. The address is 1 rue du Jeu-de-Paume, which is down the rue de Gravelle, a turning to the right off the Avenue de Sceaux, one of the three main roads joining the Place d'Armes in front of the Chateau of Versailles. (History has a habit of leading you down side streets to seek its beginnings). Then, suddenly, you are *there*. And you can feel it, in a strange unearthly way, an exciting, breathless, almost frightening way. We shall feel like that again, in other places, lovely and dreadful, and every one alive with the spirits of the Revolution.

Inside it is cool and spacious, and they will show you exactly where Bailly stood, their leader on the twentieth of June, 1789, and where each man inscribed his name on the immortal declaration. You will find Mirabeau's signature there—Mirabeau, the genius of gentle birth with an irresistible appetite for the coarse and the dangerous, the man of intellect and foresight who almost alone might have turned the Revolution into the King's hands if royalty had been only half instead of wholly blind. There his name is written for ever, with those of many more who lived and died for the new idea of liberty, equality, fraternity. As you stand before them, as you read the letters of each one, you can almost feel him standing at your side.

Coming as I did one hot summer day straight from the glories and magnificence of the Palace of Louis XIV, a few streets away, I felt most powerfully the vision and the courage which inspired these commoners to challenge the most powerful monarchy in Europe.

I had spent a day wandering through the fabulous galleries and rooms of the Palace, trying to picture the scenes which, three months after the defiance of the *Jeu de Paume*, had finally ended the life of the Royal Family at Versailles. I had stood at the head of the great staircase where the Parisians had tried to rush the Queen's apartments very early on the morning of October tenth.

You can stand, as I did, in front of the iron railings which encircle the enormous courtyard of the Palace, and recapture the excitement and fury of the Parisian mob (many of them women) as they camped in the rain all along these railings, with the uncertain, bewildered soldiers facing them on the inside. You can imagine the scene as shots rang out in the dark and men fell dead and wounded while the King and Queen and their children listened, puzzled and horrified, to the uproar outside.

The news that the crowds from Paris had arrived at Versailles and were filling the streets with noise and confusion reached the King as he was finishing a day's hunting in the forest nearby. In pouring rain he galloped back to the Palace, just before the first waves of the mob debouched into the Place d'Armes, the great square in front of it.

The King found Marie-Antoinette waiting, tense but serene. She had spent one of her strange lonely days in the Trianon, and when the alarm was given they sent an officer out to summon her back to the safety of the Palace lest some of the mob should break into the grounds behind and cut her off. In a room near the head of the stairs, with her children on either side, she had waited quietly, unperturbed it seemed, for the return of her husband, and for a moment he took her into his arms.

During the early hours of that fantastic night there was firing and shouting and much coming and going between the gates outside and the room where the King and Queen and their counsellors sat and discussed what they should do. Eventually a small deputation of the Parisian women was ushered in. To the King they said two things—that Paris was starving, and that the people wished the King to go to Paris and be with them.

At two o'clock in the morning General Lafayette arrived from Paris with a large force of militia. These, because they were of the people and wore no white cockades, were acceptable to the mob, and rank by rank they took over the guard from the hated Royalist regulars.

Now a deep quiet settled on the thousands outside. Fires were lit, meals were cooked, and the people, soaked by the earlier downpour, drowsed off to await the light of day.

Inside the Palace the guards were set and the Royal Family lay down to sleep, the King in his room, the Queen and the children in theirs. Suddenly, as it was getting light, yells and the sounds of scuffling within the Palace itself awoke the Queen. "Save yourself!" She heard a shrill cry at the door, and throwing on a gown she fled through a secret passage to the King's room; that voice, silenced in death the moment after, saved her life.

Lafayette's militia acted swiftly and bloodily, and dead and wounded figures dotted the courtyard. In a few minutes the intruders, who had found a gate unguarded in the darkness, were ejected and the situation restored. But only just, and now Lafayette was saying openly to the King and Queen that the people would not be denied, and that the safety of their lives and of their children depended on an immediate decision to leave the Palace and set out for Paris with the mob.

The King refused at first. The King of France, he said simply, could not give way to violence. With difficulty he was over-persuaded, and the order for the carriages was sent. While the horses were being harnessed and the trunks packed, Lafayette led the whole family on to the balcony in the centre of the Palace facing the main courtyard, and it was there that the mob beheld for the first time the King they still trusted and the Queen whose head they were determined to have. In tears Marie-Antoinette heard them roar; "No children! No children!," and handed them back through the glass doors behind her. Then Lafayette knelt on one knee and kissed her hand and the terrible moment was over.

You can stand below that balcony today, and picture the scene for yourself.

Soon after midday the Royal Family left Versailles forever, in a carriage escorted by triumphant harridans, headed by two men carrying severed heads on pikes, and entered Paris some hours later to the roaring of cheers and the music of hysterical people dancing in the streets.

I spent an hour or so inside the old tennis court, so quiet now, and then so pregnant. All the way back to

Paris I found myself thinking what extraordinary men these must have been to have achieved so much in so short a time, and to have devoured each other with such rapidity and brutality. That night my mind refused to let me sleep, and I was restless for the morning. I planned to go back to Versailles at early light; instead I had to return to London, and at once. (During the coming years it was often like that.)

But my imagination was on fire, and back in London I sat reading night after night about the Revolution, the men and women who made it and perished in it, how and why it came to be, and where, and when.

Whenever I returned to Paris I squeezed time and set out to find the place where some major event happened, where this man or that woman lived; then I would stand there quietly, freeing my mind from present sights and sounds. In this way I hoped I might make room for the echoes floating down to me across a hundred and fifty years, from a city ablaze with the ideas which were quickly to light flames in most of the capitals of Europe.

From the first it succeeded to a degree I had not believed possible. Each visit was more exciting than the last, and I began to know that intense emotion which Lenôtre, the master searcher, called "the first anxious moment." Is this the house? You consult your notes, bend over your 1790 map, crane up at the street name, and look around.

It is not easy, because a large part of Revolutionary Paris has disappeared; whole streets have been obliterated or diverted to make way for the great boulevards; old houses have been pulled down, office buildings and shops have sprouted on their sites. Many famous buildings failed to survive 1871, and of these the greatest loss was the destruction, in that fratricidal struggle, of the Palace of the Tuileries itself. Here was the center of the Revolution, with its memories of the flight of the Royal Family to Varennes (has fiction ever equalled this drama of loyalty, stupidity and ill-fortune?), the massacre of the Royal Swiss guards on August 10, 1792, and the roaring debates of the Convention—the Parliament of the People in the home of the Bourbon Kings.

The old rue des Cordeliers, towards which Charlotte Corday set off one hot July morning in a cab to assassinate Marat, "Friend of the People," and in which Danton and Camille Desmoulins, his pamphleteer, had their homes, disappeared altogether when they pierced the Boulevard St. Germain through; it needs time, patience, and imagination to reconstruct the picture here.

Yet much remains if you know where to look. You may still stand outside Robespierre's front door at the Maison Duplay, behind No. 398 rue St. Honoré, from which he went unsuspectingly to his frightful death. The old Cour du Commerce, which touched Danton's house, is waiting for you—smaller now than in his day, but vibrant with his memory. The Tuileries gardens are almost as they were when the Queen played there with the little Dauphin and his sister, and later when she died outside the great gates. The Conciergerie, headquarters of the Terror, is easy to find.

Above all, there is the splendid square, first called Place Louis XV, then de la Révolution, and now de la

Concorde. It has hardly changed at all—you have only to look at the prints to see that. The classic buildings on the northern side, now a hotel and Government offices, were there when the King and Queen and hundreds of their subjects died on the scaffold. Looking at these buildings, that on the extreme left is the Hotel Crillon and the whole of the building on the right is the Ministry of Marine. The guillotine was erected sometimes to the east, towards the Tuileries, and sometimes to the west, close to the beginning of the Champs Elysées. To the south the Seine flows on its even way from the Ile de la Cité to Rouen and the sea. The crowds were always thick by the bridge when the guillotine was working.

Now, if you are in the mood, we can start. But first let me introduce you to Monsieur Krok and his ancient automobile, for without these two we journey with difficulty.

ii

When you decide to embark on a search for particular streets and houses in widely different districts of a great city like Paris it is obvious that you are going to cover many miles. There is a surprising amount of what for want of a better word I will call "error-mileage"—that is, distance covered needlessly, through ignorance or wrong information. (This is often interesting, leading to unexpected "finds," and sometimes exasperating.) Landmarks such as shop names have a habit of changing owners and classification, and where you could swear there was a *Bijouterie Niçoise* at the end of a street where you had to turn right, then left, and then into an old courtyard numbered 466, one fine day your *bijouterie* obstinately refuses to appear. Instead, there is a *pâtisserie*, and you pass it by thinking, of course, that it is the next corner and not this one where you must turn. The next corner, however, stares you coldly in the face with a notary's plate outside a fusty door and window. You pass on anxiously to the next corner, with a strong suspicion that something is wrong. It is, for a garage occupies both sides of that corner!

You decide that you must have passed your landmark further back without noticing it. You retrace your steps past the notary and the window full of *éclairs* (hurry by here—I once wasted a valuable half-hour because of an irresistibly wonderful odor of hot cakes at about eleven in the morning) to the corner one before that; but no, ladies' wigs reposing on wax faces mock you this time, and you realize sadly that the jeweller has gone home to Nice, no doubt in wealthy retirement. Irrationally, you feel he might have let you know.

You stop and ponder. This is always a difficult decision to take. Shall you persevere, annoy people with your poor French and go in to ask where the offending *bijoutier* has got to, and if he ever did have his shop here, or give it up for the moment and go after your second quarry, which is a long way off on the other side of the river? Being obstinate in such things, I generally decide to go in and ask.

After I had wasted more time than I could afford—on my feet, in taxis whose drivers thought I was decidedly "odd," and in crowded buses which I never could get off—I decided I must hire a car. So I went to a garage and they sent me a beautiful Rolls-Royce with a most elegant chauffeur in a canary-yellow coat and black breeches. He had only two ideas about Englishmen who hired private cars in Paris, and both were wrong as far as I was concerned, so I said good-bye to him and tried again. This time I confided in the hotel concierge, one of that disillusioned race with crossed keys on the lapels of their frock coats and all the sin and virtue of the world in their faces, and he solved the problem for me.

"Monsieur," he said, "I know what you want. You want Monsieur Krok."

He said this with such firmness that I did not argue with him, and the next morning when I came down from my room in the tiny lift, all gilt and shiny like a cockatoo's cage, there in the hall waiting for me was

Monsieur Krok. He was tall and thin, very neatly dressed in black. In his right hand he held a folded map and a gazetteer, and in his left a soft black cap with flat shiny peak, the kind you see only on French chauffeurs' heads of the very best vintage. (Later on, when he became part of the thing he wore a beret, and no doubt felt happier in it.)

"Monsieur," he said, and bowed.

There was a quality in his voice, an elegance in his greeting, and such grace in his bow, that I knew at once he was my man.

"Monsieur Krok?" I asked.

"Monsieur, entirely at your service," he replied in English, still smiling.

I asked to see the car. He bowed once more and we went through the swing doors and down the steps outside. By the pavement stood an ancient dark blue *coupé de ville* of the type so popular in France between the wars.

Monsieur Krok opened the door with pride, and I got in.

"Where shall we go this morning then, monsieur?"

"Do you know the Place des Victoires?"

"But yes, monsieur, certainly."

"Then we'll be off," I said.

Monsieur Krok bent seriously over the high steering wheel, twiddled two or three levers mounted on its column, and we glided away, the concierge, who had come out behind us, bowing approval from the pavement.

I settled down in excited anticipation. I was on my

Marat: from a painting by Boze

3. IN SEARCH OF A MURDER

Charlotte Corday and Marat

i

At noon on a hot July day in 1793 the coach from Caen pulled up in Paris, and among the dusty passengers who climbed out was a young, well-dressed woman with auburn hair and a serious expression on her pleasant face. She was obviously new to the city, and gazed with interest at the square in which she now found herself.

Her name was Charlotte Corday, she was nearly twenty-five years old, and she had come to Paris with a fixed idea in her head—to find and kill Marat, friend of Robespierre, and editor of the violent news-sheet, *L'Ami du Peuple.*

Marat's never-ending advocacy of the most extreme terror had first shocked and then nauseated this gentle Norman girl, whose heroes were the Girondins—the orator Vergniaud, the gallant Barbaroux, the fiery Isnard, and the brilliant Madame Roland. She believed passionately in the Revolution, but for her it must be in the classic mold, noble and beautiful, built on fine ideas and set in polished phrases. She had been fascinated by the theories of Rousseau, and her conception of the sort of man who should lead the people of France forward to liberty and equality recoiled in horror at the name of Marat.

Thus it was that finally she became obsessed with the idea that it was her destiny to kill him, and she, the hater of violence, deliberately embraced it so that it should be brought to an end by her own violent act. Once the idea had taken root she was like iron in her strength to achieve it.

And now she stood in the Place des Victoires watching the men unload her box and wondering where she should find a small hotel, when one of the porters gave her a card which stated that at the Hotel de la Providence, No. 19, rue des Vieux Augustins, one Mme. Grollier had furnished rooms to let at reasonable prices. The porter told her it was nearby and offered to escort her there. She agreed, and together they turned into the old narrow

Hôtel de la Providence, rue des Vieux Augustins (now rue Hérold). Charlotte Corday's room was No. 7 on the first floor

rue des Vieux Augustins, where they soon disappeared into the modest doorway of the Hotel de la Providence.

Mme. Grollier took her in, and after she had signed the police register, Charlotte was given Room No. 7, overlooking the street from the first floor. It was poorly furnished but it was clean, and she lay down for a little after unpacking her bags. In the afternoon she sought the house of a M. Deperret, a Girondin deputy to whom she had an introduction. She wished to get his help for a friend of hers in Caen. She saw him for a few minutes only and returned to the rue des Vieux Augustins in the evening. He came to see her at the hotel the next day, when she begged him to arrange an interview for her with the Minister of the Interior. M. Deperret explained that this was impossible. He himself was already in danger of his life. The second evening in the hotel she spent writing to her family and her friends, and preparing for the ordeal she sought so deliberately.

Early on the third morning, July 13, Charlotte Corday could have been seen leaving the Hotel de la Providence and walking quickly up the rue des Vieux Augustins and the rue Coquillière, and so into the broader rue Croix des Petits Champs. She had risen soon after 5 A.M. and dressed herself carefully, even fastidiously, in a brown dress and large black hat, in pleasant contrast to her hair and light blue eyes. Modest as she was, she knew her charms and what suited her best, and she deliberately set out to make herself as attractive as she could, having heard that the "Friend of the People" was not unresponsive to women, particularly if they were young and pretty.

She hurried along towards the highway of the rue St. Honoré. It was just past six o'clock, and the only people about were porters coming from the markets and here and there a woman in a doorway or at a window. Already it was warm, the sky was cloudless, and the day gave signs of great heat later on. At the corner she turned, passing along this street until she saw the Palais-Royal on the right. Without hesitation she went through the gateway and into the gardens, where she spent some time looking at the shops in the arcades on either side, which at such an early hour were still shut. After walking round for a while, she sat down on a stone bench, until some time later the shops began to open.

At No. 177 at the Palais end of the eastern arcade, M. Bardin sold cutlery of all kinds, and here she bought a large carving knife wrapped in paper, which she hid in her dress. No. 177 is still there, near the gates.

Her purchase made, she walked once more through the gates and rapidly retraced her steps up the rue Croix des Petits Champs as far as the Place des Victoires. There was a cab rank here, and after some discussion among the drivers as to the exact location of Marat's house in the rue des Cordeliers, which this rather unusual client demanded, she got into one of the cabs and was driven down the rue Croix des Petits Champs, this time turning left along the rue St. Honoré until the driver reached the ancient rue du Roule, where he turned south towards the Pont Neuf, visible from the corner.

The cab rattled over the great bridge with its statue of Henri IV. on the right and the Ile de la Cité on the left, crowned with the towers of Notre Dame touched by the early sunshine. On the left, as it came to the corner of the Place Dauphine, though Charlotte Corday did not know it, stood the house in which Manon Phlipon, now Madame Roland, had lived as a child. As one famous woman of the Revolution passed this house in the cab to fulfil her destiny, the other was in the prison of Sainte-Pélagie, weeping for the Revolution which she had helped to lead and which had now carried her and her friends into captivity, and was soon to sweep them to the scaffold.

Nor did Charlotte Corday give a glance at the grim three-towered building a little way along the Quai de l'Horloge—the Conciergerie, in which she was soon to spend the last hours of her life.

The cab crossed the Quai des Grands Augustins into the rue Dauphine, and plunged into the maze of smaller streets and close-packed houses on the south side of the river. People were now astir, shutters were being thrown open, and children shouting with newfound energy ran from one house to another, not sparing a moment to glance at the lonely cab as it clattered over the cobbles. Past the little rue Contrescarpe, it entered now the narrower rue des Fossés St. Germain (today rue de l'Ancienne Comédie). Behind the buildings to the left lay the Cour du Commerce, which was overlooked by the back windows of Danton's house. At the top of this street, where the rue des Boucheries joined it, the driver would have slowed down to ask some passer-by where Marat lived, for they were nearly at the end of the journey.

A swing to the left past an old turreted house at the corner of the rue du Paon brought them into the dim rue des Cordeliers, and in a few more paces the cab stopped outside the entrance to No. 20, in which, on the first floor, the Friend of the People lay writing in the hip-bath which he used to soothe his endless skin irritation. The girl from Caen got down from the cab, telling the driver to wait, and going through the entrance climbed some stone steps with iron railings. In a few minutes she reappeared, and after she had asked the cabman to take her again to her hotel, she was driven back the way she had come.

She had not succeeded in gaining entrance to the house, being told by Marat's mistress, Simonne Evrard, that the editor of *L'Ami du Peuple* could see no one. As she sat back in the cab she thought calmly about her next move, for she was determined to kill Marat that day. It was stifling, and she spent the rest of it in the hotel, first writing and posting a letter to Marat telling him she had urgent news of a plot in Caen against the Revolution.

Soon after six o'clock in the evening, she set out in a cab once more for the house in the rue des Cordeliers. An hour later Marat lay dead in his bath, struck down by one tremendous thrust of her knife straight to his heart.

Throughout the dreadful scenes of blood and anguish that followed, knocked down with a chair and insulted by a howling mob in the street, Charlotte Corday never lost the air of detachment with which she had pursued her implacable way. Her composure, her bearing, and the gentle aura of nobility which was part of her, astonished all who saw her in the house, at her trial, and on her way to the scaffold the next day. So she has remained in history, on a plane of her own, above criticism or pity, the quintessence of the purest hatred applied with a virgin hand in the midst of tremendous events.

Her last letter, written in prison a few hours before her death, was to her father asking his forgiveness for disposing of her life without his permission. "It is crime which is shameful," she told him, quoting Corneille, "and not the scaffold."

Charlotte Corday: from an old lithography

ii

It was also a hot day in July when the car entered the Place des Victoires, and Monsieur Krok, after driving slowly round the lovely equestrian statue of Louis XIV, which stands in the center, drew up at the corner of the rue Croix des Petits Champs, and stopped his engine. "We are here, monsieur. Place des Victoires," he said.

I looked round. The houses are mostly offices, but the *Place* has a quiet dignity and there is very little traffic passing through to disturb one's thoughts, although it is within a few minutes' walk of the busy rue St. Honoré and almost touches the gardens of the Palais-Royal. This was my first search, and I felt the strange emotion which for me is always strong and vibrant on these occasions. I walked leisurely round the *Place*, gazing first into this courtyard and then into that, trying to make up my mind in which one the diligence from Caen had pulled up. I decided not to decide, since I did not know, and stood for a few minutes studying the locality. After a while, I felt I knew the *Place*, and could well imagine what Charlotte Corday felt and saw on just such a day as this a hundred and fifty years ago. I recrossed the road in the direction of the car, and as I passed, Monsieur Krok put down his paper and started to get out of his seat. "Not yet," I called out to him. "Don't disturb yourself." He touched his cap, smiled, and resumed reading.

I glanced up at the name of the street to make sure I was right. "Rue Croix des Petits Champs," it said clearly enough. Today it is a wide street with the Bank of France on the right, and some small shops and a garage on the left. As I passed the garage, a young mechanic was talking volubly to a girl in a pink and white dress. They were making some arrangements to go for a picnic that evening.

In a few more steps I was in the rue Coquillière.

Here my heart started to thump, and I felt that I had only to walk a little faster to overtake Charlotte Corday and her porter on their way to the hotel. I hurried down the street, which must have looked then very much as it does today, for the buildings are old, tall, and rickety and cars can pass each other only with difficulty. About twenty yards on I found myself at the corner of the old rue des Vieux Augustins, now the rue Hérold. It is narrow and cobbled, full of children, and crowded with men with hand carts and barrows. The houses, as in the rue Coquillière, are mostly old, leaning in opposite directions. Two elderly workmen, perspiring freely, and two youths were trying to coax a huge barrow, piled high with empty wooden cases, round the corner into the rue Hérold. It was with much heaving and tugging and tumult on all sides that the men kept it going; I watched them till, still shouting, they and their unstable load turned out of sight into a wide doorway halfway down the street. I thought again of that other porter and his provincial client, in whose footsteps I had entered the street only a few minutes ago.

I walked into the middle of the road. Nineteen, the number I wanted, would be about fifty yards down on the left-hand side. There were sign-boards and names in fairly large letters in that direction, and I walked towards them with a strange feeling that time had been telescoped, and that it was really 1793.

Yes, here was an hotel sure enough. An old house, painted gray (it may have been white when the paint was new), bore the looked-for number, and in large letters over the door were the words "Hotel des Victoires." I was not surprised or worried by this because new proprietors in Paris often change the name of an hotel or bar, much as in England we put in the window "Under entirely new management." The entrance was modern, with a double glass door, and I could see a small lobby beyond. There were five storeys, the top windows being in the roof. Charlotte Corday's room was, I knew, on the first floor, so it was on those windows that I fixed my eyes. They were of the usual French style, with shutters. The one on the left was half open.

I stood on the pavement opposite the hotel and took stock of the position. Here I was, looking, I thought, at the very house which had sheltered this extraordinary woman who, unknown to a soul in Paris, had arrived with holy murder in her heart. Here she must have spent that first hot evening, resting on a bed behind one of those two windows in front of me; through that doorway she had come and gone half a dozen times during the next two days; here were the paving stones her feet had trod!

I decided to go into the hotel. In the street three children regarded me with that mixture of suspicion and curiosity which they reserve for strangers.

Completely new to this business of topographical research, I had no clear idea of what I was going to ask for when I got inside, and I began to regret having left Monsieur Krok in the car. Still, the thing must be done, that was what I had come from England for, so I walked up to the door, looked through the glass, saw no one inside and entered. The little semicircular space behind the door held nothing but a round door-mat in some bright color, let into the floor. I stepped over it and pushed open an inner door with large glass panels.

I found myself in a small dark hall. On the right a door was half open, and I could see into the room beyond. It, too, was small, but light from the street was coming through the window. It seemed to be a sitting-room of some kind, and I could hear the quiet voices of a man and woman talking. Directly in front of me were the stairs. I was fascinated by these stairs. They were narrow, and led, I could see, to a small landing a little way up, curving round to reach it. There were plain iron railings on the left-hand side, and there was a little more daylight at the top. Were these the stairs up which she had followed the porter, the railings on which her hand had rested as she came down at six o'clock on the morning of the third day, on her way to buy the knife in the shop in the Palais-Royal Gardens, her mind made up? If I was right, she must have passed down these narrow stairs and over the spot on which I now stood. I closed my eyes, and in my mind I heard the swish of her dress as she went out on her terrible errand. I decided to go up the stairs.

Very softly, holding my breath, I put my foot on the first stair, my hand on the iron banister. The stair creaked loudly and the woman in the sitting-room called out, "*C'est vous, Annette?*" I paused, feeling like a burglar caught at the very beginning of his work. I made no reply and I heard her get up and come to the door. She looked up at me. She was middle-aged, of the working class, had her hair in a sort of turban, and obviously belonged to the place. I heard myself say, "*Bonjour, madame*," in a nervous, high-pitched voice, not my own, and felt myself take off my hat.

"Bonjour, monsieur," she said, adding as she saw me hesitating, "*Vous trouverez le bureau au premier, monsieur.*" She smiled pleasantly and went back into the room, and I heard the man ask who it was. I went on up to the landing feeling a little more confident. The passage from the landing led backwards over the hall, and at the end, on the right, was a door, the top half of glass with a lace curtain behind it. A girl was singing inside, the sort of half-song that women sing when they are working. I knocked gently on the glass pane. "*Entrez*," the girl's voice called at once. I turned the handle and went in.

The room was small and full of furniture; the electric light in the ceiling was on and the girl was cooking something on the other side of the room. She was young and pretty and on her head was a scarf of red and white stripes.

"Monsieur?" she queried, putting down the saucepan she had in her hand.

"Excuse me, mademoiselle," I said, "could you tell me if this house used to be called the Hotel de la Providence?"

She looked puzzled. "De la Providence? No. Hotel des Victoires, monsieur. You would like a room?" I tried again, more carefully.

"Mademoiselle," I said, "I am a schoolmaster," (I suppose I was searching for some convincing reason for my presence—I remember I had the idea that the girl might think me a little mad, and schoolmasters are generally considered to be sane), "I am looking for the room of Mademoiselle Charlotte Corday, who . . ."

"One moment, Monsieur," she cut in, "I will see for you." She turned to a desk by the wall opposite and ran her finger down the page of a large flat book lying on it. Now she understands, I thought, and is going to tell me the number of the room. I waited in suspense for her to say: "No. Seven, monsieur"—After a moment or two, during which she turned the pages back once or twice, running her finger down each, she said, still looking at the book, "I am sorry, monsieur. Mademoiselle Corday is not here—she must have left some time ago."

This anti-climax stunned me momentarily, and then I burst out laughing. The girl joined in. "She has given you the slip, monsieur?" she asked.

"Yes, mademoiselle, I'm afraid she has."

I shook myself mentally and went out into the street once more, to find the three children still there waiting for me with their quiet suspicions. I had been inside just half an hour—was it half an hour with history?

Later on I was to find out; a few months after I made this pilgrimage in the footsteps of Charlotte Corday, I found Lenôtre's account of the detailed research made by him on this very subject, fifty years earlier. Read it for yourself, for it is a model of how such things should be done. Suffice it to say that it was not in the Hotel des Victoires of my adventure that Charlotte Corday spent her three momentous days, but in a building on the other side of the street, nearer the rue Coquillière, which bore when Lenôtre found it the number 14.

Determined to make amends, the next time I was in

Paris I hurried off to see it. Alas, the housebreaker had claimed it many years before, and on its site there stands today a modern building, with a pleasant stone wall enclosing a kind of court on one side. I walked through a side door in the adjoining building No. 16 (also modern) and along a little corridor to daylight at the back. Here I found myself among old doorways and a tangle of passages which certainly are not new, and comforted myself with the thought that I had been as close to the brave spirit of Charlotte Corday as the passing years allowed.

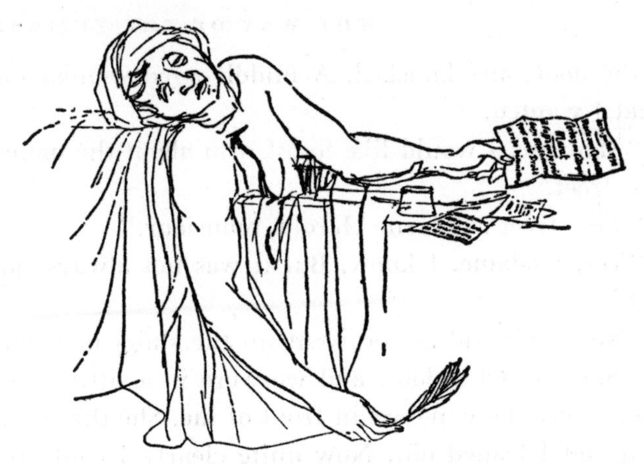

Marat assassinated: after the painting by David

4. A STREET OF PHANTOMS

i

It was in a restrained mood that I walked back towards the rue Coquillière, and again I stopped on the corner. Something made me look up at the name of the street—"rue Hérold" said the familiar blue and white enamel plate. But, what else was there? Immediately underneath, carved into the stone of the house, I could see a trace of much older lettering. Some wires were dangling down, casting a shadow. I did not want to be mistaken a second time. I looked carefully. Certainly there were letters. Now, I thought, if I could get into that building opposite and look out from the first floor window which exactly faced the name plate I could see more clearly. I went up to the door, and knocked. A middle-aged woman asked what I wanted.

"Madame, I would like to ask you about the name of this street."

"The street is the rue Hérold, monsieur."

"Yes, madame, I know. But it was not always called that."

"No?" she said as she went up the stairs in front of me. She opened a door, and we were in a sitting-room. There were the windows in front of me. She threw them open and I leaned out. Now quite clearly I could read, in the beautiful Roman lettering of the Revolutionary period, the words RUE DES VIEUX AUGUSTINS. I stood there drinking in those words, breathing the air of the old Paris of Charlotte Corday and Marat. These letters were there, the house was there, when she came round this corner that hot day in July. Her eyes had seen these very things.

I walked back along the rue Coquillière, into the rue Croix des Petits Champs, and past the big garage. The young mechanic was bending over an engine on a bench, whistling, thinking no doubt of the evening picnic with his sweetheart.

ii

The Musée Grévin, No. 10 Boulevard Montmartre, is the Madame Tussaud's of Paris, but unlike London's famous exhibition it is modestly housed in an old building with a narrow frontage squeezed between two others, and you might easily pass by without noticing it, though its name in large letters adorns the entrance hall. I had not visited it before and I was anxious to do so because a whole floor—the basement—is devoted to scenes and personalities of the Revolution, among them a reconstruction of the assassination of Marat. Moreover, the management claims that the actual bath in which he died is the one shown here, and I had to satisfy my curiosity about this.

Monsieur Krok regretted, he said, that he could not come in with me, as the police would not allow him to remain with the car in the busy street. I hurried down the stairs past one or two Revolutionary posters in glass cases, and at the bottom I asked an attendant where "The death of Marat" could be seen. He pointed to the right, and there it was, facing me.

No more startling reproduction of an historic event can ever have been made, for it is marvellously done, with that horrible sense of reality which good waxworks have.

You are shocked by it. There, with her back to the little window, stands Charlotte Corday. Her attitude is as I had always imagined it, a mixture of calm and horror, calm in that she is making no apparent effort to escape, horror in her widely staring eyes. Through a doorway on the right two women and a soldier are forcing their way in—the women are Simonne Evrard and Albertine Marat, the dead man's sister, who lived in his house with Simonne. [Actually, Charlotte Corday had walked out of the room before they burst in, and one of the men knocked her down with a chair in the little hall outside.] Facing you, on the wall, is a map of France, and above it the words "LA MORT" . . . The half light of the evening sun is coming through the window and the room is lit by it, the shadows of the figures increasing the frightening sense of reality.

A number of other visitors were gazing at the scene with their backs to me, and as I could not see the foreground from where I stood I pushed my way in among them. For a moment I failed to find the central figure; then, as my eyes fell on it, I almost jumped out of my skin. There, right beneath me, so close that I could have touched him, Marat lay white and dead in his bath! His head, crowned with a filthy rag, hangs back and partly to one side so that his half-open eyes look up at the ceiling; his face is twisted in agony; his right arm hangs limp, pointing towards the floor and to the knife stained with his blood which lies where Charlotte Corday dropped it when she drew it out of the terrible wound in his chest; on a plank across the bath are a piece of paper with some writing on it, a pen, and an inkpot.

And there is the bath itself. It is black with age and shaped like a boot, so that all of Marat's body is enclosed within it except his head and shoulders, part of his chest, and his arms. (The doctors had prescribed frequent immersion in warm water to ease the pain.)

Lenôtre, in his *Paris in the Revolution* (pp. 201-205),

has related how the bath came to be at the Exhibition. After Marat's death it went to a scrap-dealer, who sold it in 1805 to a retired General named Saint-Hilaire. He left it, among his other possessions, to his daughter, who later moved to the little town of Sarzeau, in Brittany. When she died in 1862 she bequeathed it to the local curé, and either he or his brother sold it about 1885 to the Musée Grévin to swell his depleted church funds.

I stood for a long while looking at this simple domestic piece of inanimate furniture which history had touched, and it seemed to talk, bridging the years.

"Yes, I am still here," it seemed to say. "These things really happened, and are fixed for ever."

iii

It was just before seven o'clock when the car drew up in front of the hotel. I was waiting on the steps, and as Monsieur Krok stepped out, I asked him to open his map. "Now," I said, "here is the route I want you to follow," giving him in detail the names of the streets through which we have already seen Charlotte Corday make her way in the cab. The evening was warm and airless and the streets were full of cars and taxis on their way to the centre of Paris for the restaurants and theatres. On the pavements people walked in unhurried enjoyment, and the tables outside the cafés were crowded with men and women who sat and drank, smoked and talked and eyed the passers-by.

I stopped the car on the Pont Neuf, and stood leaning on the ancient parapet. As the sun is setting, Paris is nowhere more beautiful than from one of the many bridges which span the Seine between the Chamber of Deputies [now the National Assembly once more] and the Ile de la Cité. The river glows with colour, orange, pink, red—the barges and steamers fling jet black shadows across the water, and the towers, spires and buildings stand clear against the western sky beaming shafts of light. It is old, this famous view, so many centuries of French history have passed over it. Standing here you may bid the clock stand still, and attune your mind to moods of yesterday.

We crossed to the south bank into the narrow rue Dauphine, where I called to Monsieur Krok to go slower, for the modern map showed no rue des Cordeliers, the old no Boulevard St. Germain. At the top of the rue de l'Ancienne Comédie, where it joins the Boulevard, we turned left into the hooting traffic, and I leaned out of the window, looking for the statue of Danton. This would be a good starting point, for I knew that it marked the site of his house in the old rue des Cordeliers, and I hoped to pick up the path to Marat's house from there.

In a moment I saw the statue by the pavement on the far side, and Monsieur Krok pulled the car round and drew alongside it. Resisting the temptation it held out to me (it was to be the subject of another day's search which I had in mind concerned with Danton himself) I walked eastwards, threading my way among the crowds outside the cafés.

The light was failing now, and I had yet to find the rue de l'Ecole de Médecine, which occupies the top of what had been the rue des Cordeliers. I had not far to go, for it branches off to the right from the Boulevard about fifty yards ahead, a broad backwater with a modern building on the right, and on the left a large block which from its style was either a Post Office, a Mairie, or the School of Medicine itself. It proved to be the last, and with a growing sense of disappointment I hastened towards it, for it occupied the whole of the street on that side as far as I could see. Yes, there could be no doubt about it; Marat's house, like so many others of the Revolution, had disappeared, and on or near its site the students of medicine now practised with a different technique the study and salvation of mankind.

The street was quiet, few people entered or left it, and I stood in front of the large gateway to the school with the pavement to myself, looking up at these modern walls and windows and trying to recapture something of the tremendous drama which had once been played here. So rooted was I to the spot that a voice at my side made me jump.

"You are looking for someone, monsieur?"

I turned, to find an elderly man, hatless, with grey

hair *en brosse*, and a large portfolio under one arm, looking at me with interest. No doubt he found it unusual to see someone loitering in this street at such an hour.

"Yes, monsieur. Perhaps you can help me," I answered. "Do you know if Marat lived here at one time, and is there anything of interest to see concerning him?"

The man puckered his brows for a moment. "Marat, did you say, monsieur. Was he perhaps one of the professors who worked here?"

I could not resist a smile.

"A professor," I said at last. "Yes, perhaps he was."

"Then you should come back in the morning, when the school is open. No doubt they will know of him, monsieur."

With a smile and a nod he walked away towards the lighted Boulevard, leaving me to ponder on the genius of the French people for living in the present. They do not set much store by ghosts.

iv

However, my journey to this old but much-changed corner of Paris was not unrewarded, for when I walked to the top of the rue de l'Ecole de Médecine, I found myself in the little rue Hautefeuille, and the moment I saw it I knew I was looking at walls and windows, gateways and courts which had themselves seen and heard the drama of the night of July 13, 1793.

You come on this mediaeval street without warning. The modern unemotional stone of the Medical School extends the whole length of the street which bears its

No. 21 rue Hautefeuille; old house near the site of Marat's assassination

name, and it is not until you reach the corner opposite the remains of the monastery of the Cordeliers that the old house which is today No. 21 rue Hautefeuille suddenly appears before you. It is a large building of lovely proportions, consisting of two wings, a turret and a centre block surrounding a cobbled courtyard which you enter by an arched gateway. Step in here from the pavement and you are back in Paris of the Revolution.

On the famous Turgot map of the city which Louis Bretez drew in 1739, this old house and its turreted neighbour on the corner of the rue Pierre Sarrazin are clearly shown. I looked at sheet No. 11 and there were the two wings of the gateway and the turret of the smaller house next to it. So we can be absolutely certain, in this matter of searching for old streets and houses which is so exasperatingly uncertain, that this time, with this street and these houses, we need have no doubts or reservations—they were here then as they stand today.

Let us try to recreate the scene at this corner of the rue des Cordeliers and the rue Hautefeuille as the unbelievable news spreads that a woman—"an aristo"—has stabbed the idol of the people to death in his bath less than a hundred yards away.

We hear the piercing cries coming from the open windows of No. 20, where the women watch with horror the man they love being lifted, already dead, from the bath in which the water is now a deep crimson, and the startling sound of people running pell-mell over the cobbles towards the house, shouting to each other as they run: "Marat is dead! Who killed him?"—"A filthy aristo, an enormous woman with a hatchet."—"Quick,

quick! Let us get her before she escapes." We watch them engulf the frightened coachman who brought the girl in his cab; he can be seen trying to explain to the excited men and women, now almost overturning his horse and rickety carriage, that he knows nothing about it, the girl had simply hired him as anyone might, she looked harmless enough as she sat quietly there while he drove her from the Place des Victoires on the other side of the river.

As dusk and darkness fall, the narrow streets round the house where Marat died begin to radiate the heat stored up throughout the blazing summer day. The air is lifeless, and thousands of people, half demented with rage and emotion, press and surge and sway in their endeavours to see what is happening.

For a long time, says Lenôtre, the shadows of the police and surgeons could be seen in the windows passing and re-passing from one room to another and the rumour spread that owing to the heat and Marat's disease his body was already being embalmed.

At last, after five hours, those nearest the house see Charlotte Corday, her hands bound, her hair and dress showing signs of the violence to which she has been subjected inside the house, come through the lighted doorway and stumble into the cab which had brought her there. Only with the greatest difficulty can the police and officials persuade the howling mob to make way, so that the horse can move.

Long after the shouting crowds have gone, following the cab to the prison of L'Abbaye, groups of people stand talking, arguing, weeping, in front of Marat's house and

5. THE BASTILLE

"Le quatorze juillet"

i

There is no single day in the Revolution which France remembers so faithfully as "le quatorze juillet," the National Day, on which the city streets all over the country are filled with dancing and singing people, and every town and village is gay with tricolour flags, and sashes across the ample stomachs of the Prefects and Mayors.

All this, as everyone knows, is to commemorate the fall of the Bastille on 14 July 1789, that stupendous psychological act of liberation which, in fact, freed nothing and no one other than seven blind, enfeebled or unwilling men, including two lunatics, and cost the lives of a brave and harmless Governor and about eighty people. About seventy more were wounded, including one of the garrison. Mobs crammed the little streets and the few open spaces at the eastern end of the rue St. Antoine, over which the enormous old prison, with its eight menacing turrets, had frowned for almost exactly four hundred years.

In the wild and heady air of the beginning of the Revolution, the Bastille (originally built to protect Paris from attack from the east, as the Louvre stood in the west) was regarded as the symbol of an unbearable tyranny, and its continued existence gave Camille Desmoulins, who was writing pamphlets for Mirabeau, all the powder he needed to set the crowds alight when he leaped on to a table in the gardens of the Palais-Royal on July 12 and lashed them on to the assault. (A statue stood on the spot until the Second War. Only the base remains; the Germans took the statue and melted it down.)

It was widely believed that in the Bastille hundreds of innocent people were languishing in semi-starvation. The news had just come in from Versailles that the King had dismissed Necker, his Finance Minister, on whom great hopes were placed because it was known that he had urged on the king reductions of taxation and a more liberal regime. Added to this, the story spread that the Royal German Hussars had been ordered to saddle up and ride on Paris to suppress any rioting which might follow the news about Necker.

The powder therefore was exceedingly dry, the temperature of the Parisians and of the sun in the city were at fever point, and the voice of the slim impassioned poet-agitator on the table under the trees did the rest.

"*Aux armes! A la Bastille . . . !*" In a moment the crowds were sweeping out of the gateways of the Palais-Royal and making for the arsenals. At the Invalides they helped themselves to muskets, pikes, and swords, and the sprinkling of soldiers among them laid hands on a few cannon and some ammunition with which to batter the walls and gateways of the fortress.

All the afternoon and evening of the thirteenth the crowds went roaring down the old rue St. Antoine, their ranks swelling as from every house and street more excited people joined in.

Meanwhile, in the Bastille itself, de Launay the Governor was anxiously surveying the scene from the top of the fortress, and conferring with the few officers and soldiers who formed the tiny garrison of eighty "Invalides" and thirty Swiss, with fifteen guns. No one was spoiling for a fight less than de Launay; indeed he was not only alarmed, he was astonished at what he saw boiling up beneath him, and all his thoughts were turned on how to give in to the mob below without too much indignity or downright military dishonour.

Such then was the position as the sun rose on that first "quatorze juillet." The Bourbon flag flew lazily over the great mass of turreted stonework, inside the anxious soldiers manned the parapets as best they could, the inner and outer drawbridges were hauled up, and outside the crowds cheered the sweating men who were dragging their artillery into position and pointing it at the fortress.

Suddenly, soon after eleven o'clock, the ears of the defenders caught the sound of wild cheering far below them from the neighbourhood of the outer courtyard and drawbridge. A few daring men had clambered over the roofs of the little houses nestling against the walls, and now established themselves on the hauled-up drawbridge itself. Soon they had cut its chains, and down it came. It was shortly before midday.

A leader called on de Launay to receive a deputation to negotiate the surrender of the prison. De Launay, after a hurried word with his lieutenants, agreed; the inner bridge was lowered and the deputation, which included the terrible Maillard, immediately went up and disappeared inside.

While they were parleying, the huge and excited crowds waited to see the flag lowered. As this did not happen, suspicions of treachery arose. Shouts of "They have murdered our brothers!" rang out. A few muskets went off, a cannon barked. One or two of the nervous soldiers on the parapets fired back, and immediately firing became general. Men fell dead and wounded in the people thickly massed outside the walls.

Then, as suddenly as they had disappeared, the bridge descended and the deputation re-appeared, unharmed. The firing ceased, and the men who had been inside reported that the Governor was ready to surrender to the people, on terms, which included safe custody for himself and his garrison. Otherwise, he would blow up the arsenal and the fortress with it. The offer to surrender was greeted by wild cheering, and a mass of people surged forward onto the drawbridge. Disaster ensued.

The officer on the parapet above jumped to the conclusion not unnaturally that the deputation had been over-ruled and that the mob were rushing in to butcher the soldiers. He gave the order to fire, and the leading figures on the drawbridge were at once swept away. The crowds reacted with rage and violence. [One witness, Guyot de Fléville, says, "There was a terrible uproar."] and in an instant the muskets and cannon burst once more into fire.

About four o'clock the Governor ordered the soldiers to cease fire, and sent an officer down to the drawbridge to try to restore order and to invite a further deputation to receive the surrender of the fortress, with a pledge of no harm to the garrison. By five o'clock it was all over; but before the flag fluttered down and a plain white one took its place, many of the soldiers had been cut down and shot by the mob now pouring in by the St. Antoine gate on the north-east side. De Launay was seized with two or three of his officers and brought out into the courtyard. Only the most violent efforts by two of the crowd's leaders, Hulin (later a general under Napoleon), and Elie, prevented his assassination on the spot. Eventually the little party, guarded by armed citizens, set out for the Hotel de Ville. Their respite was short, and de Launay himself was cut down and beheaded in the Place de Grève. With him perished the officers and a few faithful soldiers.

Most of the Swiss soldiers were spared on giving up their arms, and some of the "Invalides" were wildly cheered as they pinned tricolour rosettes to their hats.

Inside the Bastille parties of armed citizens roamed the damp corridors and liberated the few prisoners who came crying and blinking into the sunlight, expecting that their end had come, and for a time unable to realise that they were free.

By nightfall most of the crowds had gone home, but small parties of joyful people remained in the square, drinking and shouting in celebration of their victory.

The news that the Bastille had fallen raced through Paris and throughout France, and everywhere men and women drank and danced and sang for joy. Only the King, back at Versailles in the evening from a poor day's hunting, entered in his diary for that July 14 one word: "*Rien.*"

ii

The French have little of the nostalgic sentimentality of the British or the Americans. Not for them the careful preservation of every house and street where history has been made. Their logical minds keep them always face to face with today, and for them yesterday is often better forgotten. (If Napoleon were not forever sleeping in their midst in the Invalides he would be even more forgotten then he is.)

So it was strictly in the tradition for the Bastille, like the Temple, to be pulled down as quickly as possible; and with a thousand workmen hacking and heaving at the old stones, the towers and then the walls came crashing down amid clouds of dust and rubble which covered the roofs and floated into the windows of every house for miles around. In 1791 the last of hundreds of cartloads of stone was taken away to the Place de la Révolution, and all these were later used to build the bridge over the Seine which now separates the Place de la Concorde from the National Assembly. In this way, subconsciously no doubt, Parisians still tread the Bastille under their feet.

In 1830 there were serious riots once more in the Place de la Bastille, and again the crack of muskets filled the air. This time 380 people died for their idea of liberty, and after the revolt the municipality ordered a great column to be erected to their memory in the centre of the square. On it were inscribed, in 1839, the names of every one, and underneath, in vaults which you can see today, the victims were buried with honour and glory.

Note then that this high column pointing up from the Place de la Bastille has nothing to do with July 14, 1789. A strange idea, which seems but to accentuate the French dislike of proportionate remembrance.

iii

Monsieur Krok was disappointed when, one cold March morning, I told him to drive me to the Place de la Bastille.

"Of course, monsieur, if you wish. But there is no Bastille there now." He bowed resignedly and opened the door of the old car.

His usual keenness was gone, and I could see that he was expecting a dull morning. We sped east along the rue de Rivoli as far as it goes, and on down the old rue St. Antoine which continues it, until, at the top of a slight rise, I saw the tall column of 1839 piercing the clear blue sky, and as we approached the square which soon opened out in front of us, I called to Monsieur Krok to pull up by the pavement, and got out.

I left him grimly polishing the walnut dashboard and door fittings, and he only paused to look up and warn me once again about the danger of crossing the square on foot. I promised to be careful, and immediately forgot his existence as I pushed my way to the edge of the pavement in the huge circular emptiness which now stretched out in every direction around and in front of me.

Standing amid the rapidly circling traffic of the Place de la Bastille today, it is difficult to re-enact the famous scene unless you first compare the old street maps of that era with those you can buy at any stationers' shop today. Then, by careful study, it is possible to set out the Bastille in its relation to the modern streets and buildings. When you have done this you can let your imagination take charge, and instead of the clerks and typists hurrying into the Métro and on to the buses, the images of Élie and Hulin and Maillard and the hordes they led can take their places. The high column of 1839 becomes one of the eight towers, and with half-closed eyes you can almost see the old fortress rise again in front of you.

Now, if you stand at the end of the rue St. Antoine where it runs into the Place de la Bastille you are facing due east. On your left is the little rue des Tournelles, which was there when the Bastille fell; opposite on the other side of the square is the rue de Faubourg St. Antoine; and to your right, by the entrance to the Métro, is the Boulevard de la Bastille.

The fortress stood almost broadside on as you view the site, that is, with four of its eight towers in a line almost north to south, slightly north-west to south-east to be more exact. And it was much closer to you than the column is today.

The gate of St. Antoine, through which the mob burst late in the afternoon, was at the north-east corner, almost in line with the Boulevard Richard Lenoir of today, and the outer drawbridge, the capture of which sealed de Launey's fate, was over to the south, i.e., to your right.

Now, with a wary eye on the traffic, let us cross the open space and walk round the base of the 1830 monument. It is broader than you think, and inside are 240 steps by which you can climb to the top and stand on the little balcony directly under the winged statue which crowns the column. As you climb, in never-ending and exhausting circles, the cast-iron criss-cross of girders and plates seems to shut you in, and you notice that the iron stairs and the twisting handrail are wet with moisture. The sound of your heavy breathing and the thumping of your heart seem much too loud. Every twenty stairs or so you stop to rest.

Then, through a narrow opening, you climb out onto the balcony. At once the roar of Paris comes up to you, and your eyes swim giddily at the swirl of traffic and the scurrying crowds far below. Hereabouts, too, on that foredoomed July 4, 1789, stood de Launay, listening as you are listening, peering as you are peering. In front of you the rue St. Antoine falls away to the west, towards the towers of Notre Dame and the slender spire of St. Germain-l'Auxerrois; you can hear the noise of the buses as they rumble up the street and into the square; to the south the ugly clock-tower of the Gare de Lyon reminds you of today, but to the east, facing the site of the St. Antoine gate, the old streets and houses are as they were when the white flag flew its message of surrender only a few yards from where you stand; the rue de la Roquette and the rue de Chaventon stood where they did when the cannons roared and the crowds fell dead and wounded in the streets below.

iv

On your way back into the centre of Paris, stop at the corner of the rue St. Antoine and the little rue Jacques-Coeur, on your left as you leave the main *Place*. High up on the wall of No. 232, directly over the blue and white street name-plate, there is, for once in Paris, a memorial tablet. It reads as follows: "*Ici était l'entrée de l'avant-cour de la Bastille, par laquelle les assaillants pénetrèrent dans la forteresse le 14 juillet 1789.*"

This dingy tablet is the only thing you will find which speaks directly to you of the battle, and it seems to me appropriate enough that in the premises beneath there is a safe-depository offering protection to clients who place therein the things they value most. Just, in fact, another fortress, on the site of an older one whose fall was to be of such consequence to the future of mankind.

Monsieur Krok was standing on the pavement by his car talking to a man with a handcart of flowers when I interrupted him.

"Here, Monsieur Krok," I said, "come and see what I have found."

He shook hands hurriedly with the flower man, and we walked back together to the corner of the rue Jacques-Coeur. I pointed up to the plaque.

"What about that for the morning's search?" I said.

He gazed up at it, slowly repeating the inscription aloud. Then he made a sucking noise. "*Tiens!* Monsieur," he said with a grin and a little bow, and laid his finger along his nose. "Monsieur can smell history everywhere."

As we drove back I could see that he was happy again.

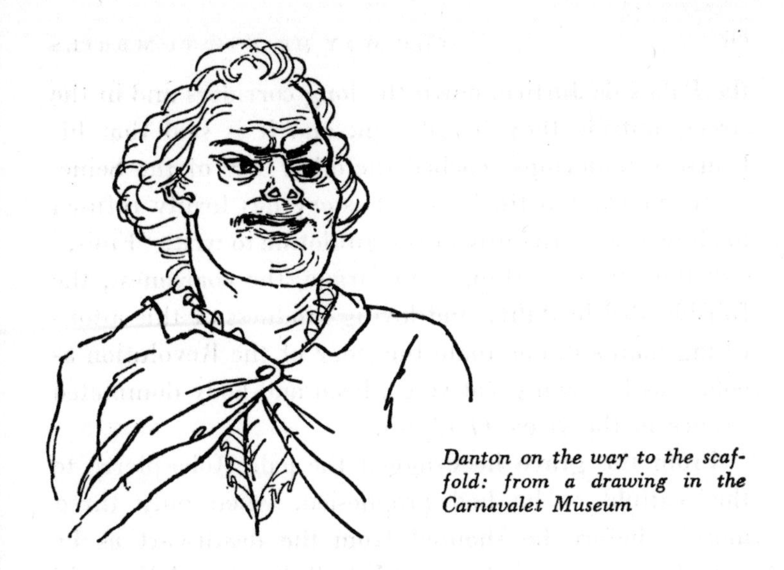

Danton on the way to the scaffold: from a drawing in the Carnavalet Museum

6. TRIBUNE OF THE PEOPLE

*"Je suis Danton jusqu'a la mort!
Demain je m'endormirai dans la Gloire!"*

i

The great names of the Revolution sound like the tocsin through the century and a half since they lived and died—Mirabeau, Marat, Robespierre, Danton.

Georges Jacques Danton, on the last day of his life when he heard his frightened judge, the despicable Herman, order the jury to retire without hearing any witnesses, stood up and with all the strength of his great lungs roared out the words at the head of this chapter. In the packed court of the Revolutionary Tribunal in the Palais de Justice, down the long corridors and in the streets outside they heard him, and it is said that his hoarse thunderings reached the other side of the Seine.

"I am Danton till I die!" History has firmly refused to allow the sharp knife of the guillotine to write "Finis," and the statesmanship, the courage, the coarseness, the full-blooded brutality and loving kindness of this astonishing man still dominate the story of the Revolution as boldly as his own great voice, head and body dominated France in the years 1792–93.

From the grave he dragged the pale Robespierre to the scaffold as he had prophesied, when only three months before he shouted from the death-cart as he passed the dictator's house: "Vile Robespierre! You will follow me soon." For Robespierre, trapped in the Convention and howled down for the first time in his life, had stood with his thin mouth open and from it no words came, with Danton's friends, led by Garnier, a deputy from his own department of the Aube, baying at him: "It is the blood of Danton that is choking you, Robespierre!"

In that little group of young men who drew up the Rights of Man, overthrew the ancient French monarchy, hurled back the armies of professional soldiers from Prussia and Austria, and let loose the Terror, Danton's physical appearance alone was enough to mark him out.

His body was thick and powerful, with a great head squat on a bull-neck, and his heavy pockmarked face depicted a man of furious energy and unchecked passion. His huge mouth seemed set in a sneer, from a tear in his upper lip when he fought a bull in his childhood; his eyes, set wide apart, were continually alive; his thick mat of hair was brushed straight back off his broad forehead; but it was his voice and the splendid mind behind it that were his most formidable weapons. When he spoke, all listened; when he laughed, everyone laughed; but when he roared no one felt safe except his closest friends.

He was born in 1759, at Arcis-sur-Aube, in the pleasant countryside south-east of Paris. As a boy he was known for his courage and vitality, fighting other boys, and bulls and pigs, with equal courage and enjoyment. He came to Paris in 1780 and set up as a petty lawyer in an obscure office near the Palais de Justice, on the south side of the river. He had no money but plenty of wit, and setting the second to remedy the first he soon got a small practice together, pleading in the courts for minor clients, reading his law books, making friends and enemies, and generally behaving as did most young men from the country who came to Paris to seek a living and if possible a fortune.

He used to frequent the modest Café de la Parnasse, No. 8 Quai de l'Ecole, a few yards from the northern end of the Pont Neuf. Soon he was paying attention to Gabrielle Charpentier, the plump, intelligent and attractive daughter of the café proprietor, and in May 1787 he married her, with a small dowry and a sum in cash from his father-in-law.

The young lawyer had become a well-known and popular figure among the clientele of the little café, always leading the discussions, bellowing coarse songs, and making love to any pretty girl he thought worth the trouble. He would stand in the street arguing with all and sundry, waving his great arms about as he laid down the law, giving offence and asking forgiveness all in the same breath.

Today, if we stand on the pavement opposite the Pont Neuf, the huge white block of a department store fills the sky, but on one side of it are old shops selling live poultry, pigeons and parrots, pots and pans, and garden tools. These houses were there when the young lawyer argued and drank and courted, and if we walk away from the river between these houses and the modern store we shall find ourselves in the old rue des Prêtres-St. Germain l'Auxerrois. Here is the Paris that Danton knew. You can see it with your eyes, and feel it coming up from the street into your bones.

The narrow houses, mostly four and five storied, have intriguing doorways leading to dark winding stairways. Inside the air is musty, the light dim and flat. Many of the dingy windows have iron grilles, and No. 11, opposite Porte 18 of the big store, has a sinister atmosphere. Nowadays it houses the lorries which ply between the warehouses and the department store, but I doubt if the swarthy porters and drivers who use it ever give Danton a thought, though they laugh, swear and talk about girls in much the same way, and almost on the very place where the Café de la Parnasse stood.

This is now the Place de l'Ecole, and in the dusk of a busy evening we can stand here and picture the burly figure bursting out of the Café, bawling his farewells with great guffaws as he rolls away to his little room over the bridge nearby.

A stream of pedestrians, cyclists, motor cars, buses

and lorries is halted by the traffic lights at the junction of the Quai du Louvre and the rue du Pont Neuf. As the lights shine green, they move forward in a blast of noise and smoke. A young man on a motor-cycle shouts over his shoulder to his friend on the pillion: "*T'as vu la petite qui sort maintenant avec Georges? Nom de Dieu! comme elle est bien tournée!*"

In this flood of homebound Parisians Danton would have been among his own kind.

ii

With the money which Danton's marriage brought him the young couple installed themselves in a flat on the first floor of a pleasant house, No. 20 on the corner of the rue des Cordeliers and the narrow Cour du Commerce. Above on the second floor lived his friend Camille Desmoulins with his wife Lucille, and the four of them often spent their evenings together. Their friendship lasted seven years, and it ended on the same day and the same scaffold, as we shall see.

All went well with Danton and his pretty wife. After a struggle the lawyer's practice grew, the flat was handsomely furnished, and two servants looked after them. Two years later their first son, Antoine, was born and their happiness was great. But it was 1789, the year of the Revolution, and that storm of ideas, action, oratory and blood swept Danton along with it, like thousands of his countrymen. In the quarter where he lived he had taken an interest in local politics, and soon found that he had a remarkable gift of rhetoric. This, with his

The Cour du Commerce as Danton would have seen it from his house

fantastic and overpowering personality, gave him quite naturally the undisputed leadership of the people with whom he associated. He founded the Club des Cordeliers, and here the great events of the day were argued and discussed, with Danton always in the head and midst of it. His fame spread, and as President of the Club, he plunged into the tempest with all his heart and mind. Soon he was to be found speaking all over Paris, denouncing the monarchy and urging on everyone the utmost determination and even brutality if necessary, to secure the liberty of the people, now released after centuries from their oppressors.

When on August 10, 1792 the mob sacked the Tuileries Palace, Danton was already an elected member of the Commune of Paris, who organised the attack on the Palace, the riots in the streets, and, perhaps, the frightful massacres in the prisons of the following month. Thus, literally overnight, the dynamic demagogue leapt to the head of national affairs, becoming Minister of Justice, with his office in a famous and lovely building still standing on the eastern side of the Place Vendôme.

There was a heroic part to play and a terrifying responsibility to be carried. Danton never hesitated, or stopped for a moment to wonder why the load should have fallen on his broad shoulders. The situation facing him and the raw revolutionary government was enough to sober them all. The war which the unworldly Girondins had declared on the Prussians and the Austrians over the safety of the Royal Family was going all to pieces, and that summer the invading armies stood as near to Paris as Verdun, a bare hundred miles away.

Three Frenchmen were determined that the enemy should be stopped and expelled from French soil—Danton, Carnot and St. Just. The energy and oratory of the first, the organising ability of the second, and the cool military insight of the third were lashed together in unceasing endeavour for the salvation of the Revolution. Their flaming new belief that Liberty, Fraternity and Equality must sweep the world inspired them, and night and day they grappled with the impossible.

The story of the creation of the Republican armies, their ranks filled with ardent young men anxious only to conquer or die, of the call to arms which went out all over France, of the harnessing of every workshop, large and small, that could churn out guns and muskets, swords and bayonets, cannon balls and bullets, clothing and equipment, is the greatest of all the astonishing achievements of these pulsating years. And it was Danton who gave it voice and purpose and direction. Listen to him, with the enemy almost at the gates:

To Roland, a fellow Minister who spoke of the wisdom of moving the Government from Paris: "Do not mention flight too loudly, citizen. The people might hear you!"

To the Convention: "We demand that everyone should fight. Some must guard the frontiers, some shall dig trenches, and others must defend our cities with pikes and axes. I say that anyone who refuses to aid France at this moment of history must be punished with death. The sound of the tocsin is not the signal of alarm —it is the sound of the charge which will destroy the nation's enemies. Rather than surrender Paris, let us fire the city with twenty thousand torches!

"I tell you, it is daring, more daring, and always daring which will save France!" [The famous words translate poorly. How render into another language, these?: "*Pour vaincre des ennemies de la Patrie, il nous faut de l'audace, encore de l'audace, et toujours de l'audace!*"]

The effect on the anxious members of the Convention was miraculous. They stood and roared their applause, and went out from that session to spread the news that all was at stake, that it was to be a battle to the finish and that revolutionary France would win. Danton had said so.

As one reads the glowing words of this man of violence we can agree with Michelet that "on such occasions, words and deeds are alike. Danton's words were France's energy made concrete, a cry from the nation's heart." * The similarity between the Danton of 1792 and the embattled Winston Churchill of 1940 stands out as something more than a coincidence. De Gaulle's brave words: "France has lost a battle, but she has not lost the war" are also in the Danton tradition.

The raw troops flooding to the front were led by commanders most of whom had literally been stamped out of the ground. There were Hoche, Kléber, Pichegru and others like them, who later led the eagles of Napoleon to victory all over Europe; professional soldiers like Kellerman and Dumouriez lent their skill and experience to

* Translation by Madeleine Boyd from Henri Béraud's *Twelve Portraits of the French Revolution* (Grant Richards & Toulmin.)

Danton's massive heaving. Thus were the invaders overthrown at Valmy and Jemappes, and thus was France miraculously saved.

iii

Danton resigned from his public office soon after the September massacres, for which he must bear some of the responsibility. Despite his gift of leadership, he did not like governing, preferring to be "a plain representative of the people," his own words.

"I am sick of life," he said on the eve of his trial. "Better to be a poor fisherman than try to govern men."

For months he had lived only for France, and the stones of the Cour du Commerce had not echoed with his footsteps for many a day and night. Gabrielle, with the two little sons (a second had been born in February) watched helplessly the wreck of her happiness and her marriage as the tornado she still loved found time only for his tasks, and now for other women. While Danton was away in Belgium on the nation's business, she left the Place Vendôme, which had always oppressed her, and returned to the house in the rue des Cordeliers. There she died in September, her part played, her short life given to the man who had roused France to victory.

On hearing the news Danton tore back to Paris, shattered. So wild was his grief, so uncontrolled his refusal to believe that she was dead, that he had her body dug up from the earth for a last embrace, and on the spot he ordered Deseine, a deaf-mute, to take her death mask so that he might have something to keep of the wife he had forgotten.

Throughout the winter and spring he laboured on, inspiring the doubters, threatening the cowards; but now he despaired in his heart, not for France, but for his belief that this thing called liberty was worthwhile if the only way to win it lay through a worse tyranny than before.

Still, in April 1793, he allowed himself to be elected to the all-powerful Committee of Public Safety. Immediately the long grapple with Robespierre began. No two men fighting for the same cause could have been more different, save that both were lawyers. Danton was all heart and passion; his neat little colleague never allowed a public word to pass his lips that had not been written and re-written beforehand. At first Danton dominated the Committee by his moderation and his old powers of persuasion, but gradually he found himself more and more opposed to the cold-blooded policies which Robespierre consistently advocated in his thin voice. In July Danton resigned once more, and this time for good.

The sudden decision to break with it all was typical of the man. Everything must be done to the utmost; half measures were not in his make-up. So now, weary and disillusioned, his own countryside at Arcis-sur-Aube began to call powerfully to him. To Arcis therefore he must go, and at once. He knew that the war, though not over, was won, and already he could sniff through those wide nostrils of his the stink of the Terror to come. He was for none of it. "I do not find myself," he said, "a friend of Marat."

The year before, Danton had bought a fine house with some land in the town of his birth, and now, shutting up the little household in the rue des Cordeliers, he left at last for Arcis. [I visited the site in 1955. A new house stood there—Its owner, M. Robin, whose grandfather bought Danton's house from his sons, told me that it was destroyed in the fighting in June 1940. The park and the gateway which Danton erected are still there.] With him went his second wife, Louise Gély, a girl of sixteen, whom Danton in his loneliness had married four months after Gabrielle's death. The two girls had been friends, Louise's father being a regular client at the Café de la Parnasse. Now he was a minor official in the Ministry of which Danton had been the head. Louise was terrified of the public god she had married, and all the tenderness and devotion he pressed on her failed to soften these feelings.

During those autumn months the man of the people

lived the life of a countryman, enjoying his new property and adding to it, entertaining his local friends, and talking of the new life he meant to make for himself away from Paris and the turmoil he had done so much to create.

Occasionally a grim echo from the city would reach him, as when, in October, a friend burst into his dining room one evening to tell him the news that the Girondins had been sent to the scaffold—Vergniaud, Brissot, and most of the fine intellects that had helped to call the Revolution into being.

Danton jumped from the table, his face disfigured, his voice thick with rage. "These madmen!" he roared. "They will kill us all before they are finished." Then he sank down, his great head in his hands, and spoke no more that evening.

iv

The Girondins had gone to the scaffold singing the Marseillaise, with Vergniaud coining his famous "The Revolution, like Saturn, devours all its children." The ruthless men of the Mountain, so called because they sat in the upper galleries of the Convention, whose leader was Robespierre, took full advantage of Danton's absence from the scene. Despite the fact that Paris—and for the moment, France—was freed from the invading armies pledged to restore the Bourbon rule, at their command the gaunt shape of the guillotine still stood and worked in most of the great cities of France.

Many of the victims had committed no other crime than to be of gentle birth. Personal vendettas and the basest motives passed easily into "judicial processes" in the icy hands of the Public Prosecutor, Fouquier-Tinville, who saw to it that the Revolutionary Tribunal, sitting daily in the Palais de Justice, was never short of work.

News of all this reached the tired man at Arcis-sur-Aube, and not only of this but of a tide most personal to himself. By letter and by word of mouth his friends warned him that Robespierre and St. Just were moving powerfully against him, spreading rumour spiced with half-truths that Danton's disapproval of the continuing butchery was because of fear that his own duplicity was about to be unmasked.

To these warnings Danton at first paid no heed. "Tell Robespierre," he growled, "that I will crush him in the palm of my hand when I think it necessary." But as the weeks passed, the pleading of his friends became more insistent. Their own lives as well as his, they told him, were now in danger. He must return to Paris or flee the country. Danton rounded on them for that. "Can a man take his country with him on the soles of his feet?" he cried.

In the end he saw clearly that he could remain outside events no longer, and that his idea of a new life—as though the Revolution and his part in it had never been—was impossible. These last happy weeks fishing and pottering round his beloved house and fields were prizes he could not keep; he had washed his hands in too red a stream, breathed too strong a blast on the fires of the Revolution. In his heart he knew it, and roused at last to the reality of his position ("Robespierre would arrest *me?*" he had said, and laughed. "Let him dare. He could not boil an egg properly!") he left Arcis for the last time in mid-November, and on the twenty-sixth was speaking once more in the Convention.

All over Paris, all over France, the news of his return came like the blast of a trumpet. The small-minded, the mean, the cowardly, the cronies of the Incorruptible, felt it and shuddered. The masses were happy, and showed it, crowding in to hear him, feeling safer with him among them. His friends began to hope once more.

In the Convention Danton made a statesmanlike defence of a number of people whom he thought innocent of charges brought against them, pleaded for vigour, yes, energy, yes, but called for a halt to the extremes which, he argued, were now unnecessary and even dangerous for France. He asked for moderation, except for those who had no claim to it.

Robespierre, in a masterly combination of hypocrisy and guile, seemed to agree with him, and there was a flash-in-the-pan reconciliation between the two. But there were many who noted shrewdly the neat way in which Robespierre had not committed himself, the seemingly casual fashion in which he had spoken of Danton's qualities being proof against the calumnies spoken about him. Thus he began to sharpen the knife for his former colleague's neck, with a mixture of slimy compliments and vague references to "accusations." Others noticed that Danton, despite his rest in the country, seemed tired of these endless debates, with their personal quarrels and manoeuvres.

None the less, he defended his ideas with all his old skill. "I am for the Terror!" he said, "but let it be directed only against the real enemies of the Republic." Thus by inference he attacked the system which was sending an ever-growing number of unfortunates to the scaffold, many of them completely unknown. To him now the spectacle of prostitutes, grandmothers, nuns, and ex-servants of the old order, whose only crime was to have said at some unguarded moment: "The King was a good Citizen," filling the carts on their way to the guillotine was not merely stupid but degrading to a revolution which had as its charter the Rights of Man. A year earlier he had no such qualms, but blood had sickened him.

At times he acted with energy, as when he inspired Camille Desmoulins to write his brilliant *Le Vieux Cordelier*, in which everything that Robespierre stood for was pilloried in glittering satire. So great was its effect that men stood in queues to get a copy. The unstable poet was to pay for it with his head when Robespierre felled his leader.

More than once Danton's coarse wit set the deputies roaring—and always at Robespierre's expense. The man of virtue had spoken for over an hour on Virtue, Virtue *à la Robespierre*. Bored with it, Danton threw this at him: "I know of no better virtue than that which I practice nightly with my wife!"

Had he wished, Danton could yet have been reappointed to the Committee of Public Safety—indeed, so great was his reputation and so little diminished his influence now that he was back in Paris that there is little doubt he could have taken the leadership into his own hands. But it meant sending Robespierre and his friends to their deaths, and at once, and Danton was in no mood for bloodletting.

"I will join no more Committees," he cried. "Rather, I will be the spur of them all!" This infuriated Robespierre, and, half-frightened himself, he determined to strike as soon as he dared.

Thus Danton entered the last weeks of his life. More and more it became obvious to his friends that either he did not realise the plot closing in on him and them, or he did not care.

By the end of March the net was drawn tight. On the thirty-first, St. Just, speaking in the Convention with all the clarity and effectiveness that had put him where he was, delivered a broadside of charges against Danton of the gravest kind. He had embezzled the State's funds, he had taken bribes from foreign enemies, he had deliberately left Paris to plot against the government, and by his speeches he had shown that those whom the justice of the people wished to strike could always rely on him to defend them. Therefore, by order of the Committee of Public Safety, Danton had that night been arrested. The voice was St. Just's, but the brief was Robespierre's, drawn up with all the care and cunning which was second nature to the lawyer from Arras.

At first the deputies, except those few in the know, were incredulous, some openly hostile. St. Just paid them scant attention, steadily developing his case against the man whose very existence, he declared, was now a mortal threat to them all. Such was his quiet eloquence, so damning appeared the charges and the evidence for them, so clear was the indication that anyone who opposed was himself ripe for the scythe, that soon only Legendre, a Dantoniste, dared to speak in his defence. He proposed that Danton, because of his past services to the nation, should be summoned to appear at the bar of the Convention. He, Legendre, felt sure of the result.

As he spoke, Robespierre slid into the chamber, and in a passionate speech demolished Legendre and the few with courage enough to think like him. No one else, declared the Incorruptible, had been given the privilege of avoiding the Courts when charged with treason. Why Danton? Which was the more important—France, or one man?

It is said that Robespierre—usually so toneless and inhuman—in this speech displayed a fire and violence that surprised everyone. The reason is clear. Robespierre knew that if Danton was allowed to speak freely in his own defence it was he, Robespierre, who would "look through the little window." It was now or never, and he meant it to be now.

His speech settled the issue beyond doubt or argument, and the mighty assembly of the people, the instrument of the Revolution itself, went out of the building mumbling with fear, thinking of the burning words Danton had spoken to them, and the great things he had done so short a while ago; and all knew that they would neither hear nor see him there again.

V

The night before, as Danton sat before a bright fire in his study overlooking the Cour du Commerce, his wife Louise apprehensive and silent at his side, the orders were signed and sent out for his arrest.

All that evening he had said very little, and was restless. He knew he was being violently attacked in the Convention, yet he deliberately stayed away. For the first time inertia held him in face of danger, this time personal. That very day friends had pleaded once more that he should leave Paris while he could. "Now, Danton, tonight!" And he had made no move.

Very early in the morning armed men came to the street outside his house. At the sharp noise of their boots and their muskets on the cobbles, Danton said simply: "They have come for me," and rose to meet the officer who was already climbing the stairs. Deliberately, with no attempt to use his great physical force to obstruct what he well knew was the beginning of the end, he said goodbye to his wife, now crying and trembling, went down the stairs to the waiting soldiers, and in a few minutes was lodged in the Luxembourg Prison nearby.

If there was a wind blowing that night down the narrow Cour du Commerce, and into the rue des Cordeliers, it must have caused the lamps to waver in their old brackets as Danton left his home to go before that Revolutionary Tribunal which he himself had set up to strike at the enemies of the nation.

Danton's statue

7. A HEAD TO REMEMBER

i

In 1876, when the Boulevard St. Germain was cut through the old streets south of the river, the rue des Cordeliers disappeared and with it No. 20, Danton's house. Lenôtre, *Paris in the Revolution*, p. 234 et seq., and Belloc, *Danton*, p. 329 et seq., have given detailed and fascinating descriptions of the pleasant rooms, the pretty wallpaper and the furniture of the Danton ménage. These should be studied by those who visit the site today, for they give an intimacy and reality to the man whose fine statue, almost on the same spot, we can find without difficulty.

Cross the Pont Neuf, go over the Quai des Grands Augustins, and keep straight on down the rue Dauphine until it becomes the rue de l'Ancienne Comédie [the same route as in Chapter Four]. On your left is the eleventh century rue St. André des Arts. Walk a few steps down this street, and there on your right over an archway you will see the words: "Cour du Commerce."

I know many old streets and houses in Paris, but in none do I ever have quite the same feeling of excitement and anticipation as in this long narrow clutch of houses and doorways, windows and shutters, stone stairways, old water-taps and hanging iron lanterns.

Nothing is changed here since Danton brought Gabrielle Charpentier to their new home at the far end of the Court in 1787; in the sunlight the shadows fall as the two lovers saw them when they walked arm-in-arm to do their shopping or to visit her parents in the Café de la Parnasse; when it rains the wet light glistens on the same cobble stones; and at night, when the irregular lamps shine along its darkness, they throw into shadow and relief the shapes and outlines of all the nights that Danton lived here, and of that early morning, before sunrise, when the sound of the tramping soldiers woke up the people in these houses, shot windows up and heads out, and sent the scavenging dogs frightened into the Cour de Rohan. Here, of all the places in Paris where the men and women of the Revolution lived, loved, hated, fought and died, your eyes are seeing what they saw, your feet are standing where theirs stood; it is a place to be quiet in, to take time over, for here time has stood stock-still.

The first part of the court is roofed with glass. Walk slowly by the old shops in this tiny arcade, painted a lovely blue and white when I last saw them. They have long and narrow windows with beautifully curved tops, and the frames are all of wood. The laundry at the end stands behind some lovely iron railings, and in the window of the furniture-maker there is often an old sofa or armchair upside down, just as the craftsman has left it to go for his lunch. There is a shop which sells brushes of every shape and size, whose proprietor seems ageless himself as he sits on the wreck of an old iron chair and surveys his little world. I have often wondered about that chair. . . .

Over another shop rows of butchers' hooks set you thinking, and outside the little café by the archway the twentieth century has been ungracious enough to announce that inside one may find: "*Activités du Sporting Club du 6 ième*." Brave new world to enter here!

Now walk on, and to your right and left are the houses in which Marat set up and printed his ferocious *L'Ami du Peuple*, a proof of which he was correcting when Charlotte Corday stabbed him to death in his bath in the flat two hundred yards away. No. 8, on the left, is still a printing works, and piles of modest dance programmes and theatrical bills were stacked in one of its windows the last time I was there. You can stand outside with the *click-clack* of its ancient presses sounding in your ears, and it does not need much in the way of imagination to let you see, in the dim light through the open door-

Printing office in the Cour du Commerce where Marat produced his ferocious newspaper l'Ami du Peuple

way, the livid face and squat figure of Jean-Paul Marat urging the printer to give him still more copies of his bulletin of hate.

Almost opposite No. 8, on the corner of the way out into the rue de l'Ancienne Comédie, is an old shabby three-storied house. It faces three ways; iron railings run above the gutters, and iron bars enclose the large window in the centre on the ground floor, giving it a sinister appearance. I was told locally that it was in this house that the humanitarian, Dr. Guillotin, set up his first "machine" as an experiment and chopped off the heads of nothing more revolutionary than a few sheep. The thing worked, and the doctor persuaded the Convention that by this method death would be both painless and instantaneous. They adopted it, and the story goes that its inventor was later to find out for himself just how painless and instantaneous it really was. A piece of poetic justice, if true; but it is untrue. The doctor died in his bed in 1814, saddened by the terrible use to which his machine had been put. (Chamber's *Encyclopaedia*, vol. vi, pp. 637-38).

Be sure to go into the Cour de Rohan, on the other side. Here some of the walls and stairways date back to the early middle ages. The courtyard is the site of an old bishop's palace, having associations with Rheims and Rouen. ("Rohan" is an older spelling.) There is a well with an ancient pulley outside one of the houses at the far end; the only sounds in this place are domestic, as are the pungent smells emerging from kitchens, sculleries, and "the usual offices," in pleasing French conglomeration.

Certainly anyone standing here gossiping in the cool of a summer evening in 1790 would have heard, from the Cour du Commerce, the voice of Danton as he passed the time of day on his way home, and his laughter would have come clearly on the soft air. In this place you seem very close to it, and to the tears of his deserted Gabrielle.

Let us go back now to the Cour du Commerce, and walk up to the far end, through the archway of the modern building above. Outside is the busy Boulevard St. Germain, and exactly opposite is the statue of Danton.

Here the tribune of the people stands, his right arm flung outwards, one leg forward, the other back, so that his great chest is thrown out and his whole body braced and vibrant. His left hand rests on the shoulder of a child, and under his right an armed and eager citizen looks up to him for orders. The whole group perfectly portrays the man—his great physical presence, his burning patriotism in the proud lift of the head, the finger stabbing the air, his booted feet planted firm as a rock on the soil of France, and his wide-collared coat flung out and back by the movement of his body as he speaks. In his splendid face the eyes seem to blaze, the great brow to glisten with sweat. On the plinth the call for "*l'audace*," word for word as he hurled it at the Convention when the enemy were at the gates, reminds the passer-by of the spirit of the man who demanded nothing less than victory. "*Vaincre, ou mourir!*"

The house from which he was taken on the night of March 30, 1794, stood about twenty yards to the east of the statue, where the present rue de l'Ecole de Médecine joins the Boulevard. I have stood there often, by day in the centre of a fast stream of traffic of every kind, and late at night when only an occasional car or van disturbs the silence. A few people pass to and fro in the Cour du Commerce, where the dim lanterns still cast their queer shadows; and I find myself wondering how near is 160 years ago? How far away is yesterday?

It is then that Monsieur Krok touches me on the shoulder, and reminds me that it is midnight, and therefore almost tomorrow.

ii

The trial of Danton and the little group of men arrested with him lasted three days, and sentence of death, to be carried out the same day, was read to them in prison on the morning of April 5, Danton refusing to listen. Many fine accounts of this landmark of the Revolution have been written. Among the best are Belloc: *Danton*, p. 259 et seq.; Lenôtre: *Tribunal of the Terror*, p. 136 et seq.; Hermann Wendel: *Danton*, p. 353 et seq.; J. B. Morton: *The Bastille Falls*, p. 250 et seq. As the reader can so easily and with such benefit turn to them I will here attempt no more than an outline.

Robespierre and Fouquier-Tinville had taken the utmost care that nothing should go wrong. The judge, Herman, was a creature of Robespierre's who knew that one mistake on his part would cost him his life, while the jury of seven were hand-picked and thoroughly "instructed" before and during the trial.

Despite this, things went all in favour of the accused during the first two days. Danton's sallies at judge and prosecutor kept the crowds in the public part of the hall in a constant uproar of laughter and derision; even the jury were shaken, and showed it. As time went on Herman and Fouquier became more and more anxious and angry. Finally, sweating with fear, they took refuge in one of the most despicable tricks in history.

The accused were insistently demanding that witnesses should be produced to prove the allegations made against them, and that their own witnesses should be called in their defence. This Robespierre was determined to prevent, and he had given the strictest orders to judge and prosecutor, for Danton at any time was dangerous, but Danton on the attack would demolish a hundred false witnesses and walk out of the courtroom a free man and a public hero.

The very thought struck fear in Robespierre's heart, and when he received a hurried note from Fouquier saying that the trial was "out of hand," that the public were cheering Danton and his friends and that "fresh instructions were required" by his now thoroughly alarmed lieutenants, he sent St. Just in haste to the tribune in the Convention to swear that the prisoners, wild with guilty fear, were "obstructing the Court and making the course of justice impossible."

"We have all been saved in the nick of time from a wicked conspiracy," St. Just declared. "It is the nation which is in peril." Therefore, to protect the people he proposed an immediate new decree, that anyone who impeded the course of justice, or who insulted and resisted the law, should there and then be pronounced *hors de débats*, to be condemned without further waste of time. The frightened deputies agreed, and a message was sent at once to the Court giving Herman his new and terrible authority.

"Here is something to help you," said the man who brought the letter. "We need it" was all that the thin-lipped prosecutor had time to reply, for they had been forced to sit helpless for nearly three days while Danton and his friends tore the prosecution to shreds.

"You may kill me, but you shall not insult me!" Philippeaux had cried. Westermann, a commander straight from the front, had torn open his shirt and bellowed: "See, people! I have received seven wounds for France in front; this is the first I have ever had in the back!"

Danton, catching sight of police spies whispering among the jury, had called them "cowardly butchers," and on being ordered by Herman to keep silent when he rang his president's bell, shouted with laughter and called out to the crowd: "A man on trial for his life takes no heed of a little bell. He roars!"

But it was soon over. Armed now with what he wanted, at Fouquier's request Herman closed the session for the day, and when next morning the prisoners began once more to demand witnesses the fatal decree was read out. In a stunned Court the judge asked the jury if they were "satisfied." They were, they said, and retired to consider the verdict that everyone now knew was inevitable. They were not away long, and when they returned announced that all were guilty.

A terrible scene followed. Desmoulins tore up his defence and hurled the pieces at the judge's table, while Danton roared: "My name is on every revolutionary decree! Produce your witnesses, and I will tear the mask from these vile imposters and deliver them to the people for vengeance!"

Still shouting, clinging to the benches and tables, the prisoners at last were overborne and taken at once to the dark prison of the Conciergerie next door. It was the last stage.

The house of Madame Roland on the south side of the Pont Neuf

iii

The genius and the courage of Danton never shone more brilliantly than on this the last day of his life. To his friends condemned with him he gave strength and comfort in the way most needed by each of them.

It was four o'clock when they went up into the tumbrils and out into the evening sunshine of a warm April day. The carts passed along the Quai de l'Horloge, in front of Mme. Roland's house, and over the Pont Neuf to the other side of the Seine. Danton stood throughout the two hours' journey to the scaffold. Without apparent interest he passed close by the Café de la Parnasse, and seemed not to notice the crowds of dazed Parisians who filled the streets to see him go by.

Desmoulins, clutching a lock of Lucille's hair, was wildly calling on the people to save him.

"Pay no heed to these riff-raff," cried Danton, and gradually the free-lance of the Revolution recovered a calmness which he preserved to the end. His last letter to Lucille, in which he begged her: "Do not call to me, for your cries would tear me apart in the grave" is one of the tragic love letters of the world. You may read it in the *Bibliothèque Historique*, 29 Rue de Sévigné, near the Carnavalet Museum. Fabre d'Eglantine, the actor, was blubbering because he had written some verses and was afraid a rival would steal them. To him Danton replied with a pun to turn the stomach. ["*Taisez-vous! Dans une semaine vous aurez assez de vers.*" ("Quiet! In a week you will have worms enough.")]

Through the little streets that lead by twists and turns

into the long rue St. Honoré the carts jolted slowly forward. The crowds were thicker than ever before. Except for his outburst as the procession passed the Maison Duplay, where Robespierre sat white-faced behind closed shutters, Danton kept up a stream of jokes, songs, and words of encouragement to the others in the tumbril with him.

He was the last to mount the guillotine. Just before, at the foot of it, he had embraced Hérault de Séchelles, a man of noble blood, a soldier. The executioner's assistant tried to part them. "Fool!" cried Danton, "do you think you can keep our heads apart in the basket?"

When they had all gone, each one sustained by his presence, he walked up the steps firm and erect and for a moment looked far over the heads of the crowd. Then to Sanson, the executioner: "Show my head to the people. It is worth it." As the knife fell, a great sigh rose from the stupefied thousands who had watched him die.

He was thirty-four years old.

Robespierre

8. HOUSE OF THE TERROR

i

Robespierre—

The name in any language spells tyranny. Ask the next man you meet who was the most heartless, cruel, and cold-blooded figure in that cascade of death which is called "The Terror," and he will probably answer "Robespierre." For over a century and a half his name has stood for the personification of the tyrant and the mainspring of the Revolution. So it will remain.

History is as difficult for the ordinary man to unravel as truth is to define, and the deeper he digs among the facts and manuscripts, and the books to which they have given birth, the harder it becomes to chart the maze with certainty. The centuries roll by, new facts appear from time to time unknown to writers of an earlier age, casting a light where shadows fell before, or putting out the light where men have thought they saw it. When this happens, more books appear, old controversies long since dead blaze again. The smoke eddies this way and that, smirching names that hitherto seemed clean.

But not, you would say, with Maximilien Robespierre? His whole short life, ended when he was thirty-six, lies before us; document after document, letter after letter, speech after speech—all are there for our inspection, and books enough to fill a cupboard. Certainly, like all revolutionaries, for him the end justified the means.

Here was a man sprung from no "family." He was born and brought up in a small town in the north, trained as a lawyer and practising in his native Arras when the storm broke in 1789. He had a local reputation for priggishness, he was cold and he was dull, and like all his kind, over-sensitive about his dignity. Humour he did not know, except when, his cheeks burning, he heard laughter in the court at his expense. Yet he was not without his briefs, being accurate, well-read, and above all incredibly persistent and consistent; he kept droning on in his high-pitched voice, looking always straight before him, boring his way into the vitals of the case like a human gimlet.

Then, at thirty-one, he was elected to the States-General soon to meet in Versailles, the first for 175 years, and that year, 1789, saw him setting out from Arras to join the flood of others of his generation who from all over France were gathering to rescue the country from the pit of bankruptcy and ill-humour into which it had fallen. Like many others, he too had read deeply of Rousseau's philosophy, and the Ideal State to which all mankind should aspire appealed strongly to his orderly, logical mind. So he took his place among the grim delegates of the Third Estate, determined to make his name, to be heard, to do, and to compel others to do likewise.

At first he failed. In all those hundreds he was but one, unknown and dismally unattractive. Besides, he got little chance to show what he was made of, and when, in October of the same year, the King was forced to return to Paris from Versailles, the National Assembly (as it had now become) following him, the provincial lawyer found himself in the capital with nearly every rung of the ladder still to climb. For two years more, till 1791, he continued as he had begun, living in cheap lodgings in an unpretentious street near the Temple, [No. 64, rue de Saintonge—The street is still there, but only the lower front of the house remains] making no substantial mark outside the Jacobins Club, where they were beginning to listen to the little man who seemed able to keep his mind off trivialities and his eye on the target, Rousseau's Ideal State.

The change came in July of that year. The flight to Varennes and recapture of the Royal Family had split men into opposing camps—those who were for the immediate overthrow of the King, and those who opposed it or were not yet ready for it. On the Champ de Mars, on July 17, violence had broken out between Lafayette's militia and the ordinary people, and men, women, and children lay dead because of it. A reaction set in against the extremists, and Danton had to fly to England. The members of the Jacobins, Robespierre among them, went in fear of their lives.

Characteristically, he had advised caution and spoken against violence, the careful lawyer remaining uppermost. He was returning home that night, the seventeenth, through streets full of danger, when a fellow member of the club, a well-to-do master-carpenter or cabinet-maker named Maurice Duplay, spoke to him, offering to give him a night's shelter at his house nearby, No. 366, rue St. Honoré, today No. 398-400. This man, Duplay, had listened with growing admiration to the lawyer from Arras, and without doubt felt at that moment two emotions—one a genuine anxiety for Robespierre's personal safety, the other a desire to make himself important by having in his modest family circle the young orator from the Jacobins. Robespierre accepted his offer, and that night slept in the cabinet-maker's house. It was to be his home till the end.

It was, as we have seen, July 1791. He had almost exactly three more years to live, three years during which he raised himself by his thin, penetrating oratory, his icy reasoning, his fanatical belief in his own capacity to know what was right for the country, and finally his blind, ruthless drive through blood and terror for his Ideal State, to the position of Dictator of France, hated by all Europe, openly feared and secretly execrated by millions of his countrymen. Only a few men could he then call friends—the young, brilliant, brave St. Just, who was to sacrifice himself for Maximilien, the crippled Couthon (these two were fellow-members with him on the all-powerful Committee of Public Safety), young

Philippe Lebas, member of the Convention, who killed himself at Robespierre's side, and his own younger brother Augustin, who died with him on the scaffold. Only in the Maison Duplay, which we shall shortly visit, did he find something more than friendship; personal comfort and safety, flattery and admiration, the faces and voices of women who idolised him, and the soft fragrance of a girl who loved him.

Such was Robespierre, whose name is forever linked with the greyest horrors of a convulsion that marked the end of one world and the beginning of another.

In all revolutions, except perhaps in England, blood is bound to flow before the issue is resolved. When the dust of turmoil has settled, the conflicting figures stand out more clearly, and we may judge them better.

Was Maximilien Robespierre a terrorist by nature, by necessity, or both? Those who believe the first will cite his implacable hatred of the intellectual and spiritual Girondins, whom he drove first from office and then to their deaths; the vile and merciless trickery with which he secured the heads of Danton and Desmoulins, his friends a year earlier; the evil "Law of Prairial" which he signed deliberately, knowing that with it the words freedom and justice passed out of the vocabulary, and stark terror took their place.

Those—Hilaire Belloc among them—who hold to the second, see in him a man so rigid, so priggish, so bigoted, so suspicious, that he could cherish only one objective—the pure Republic where men are equal, and all equally good—or must be made to be so. With this vision ever before him he became blind to all else. When he was struggling upwards to power, he was ruthless to achieve it; all-powerful, he was terrible to perpetuate it.

In the end, he was destroyed by a few men less honourable, less upright, and of far smaller moral stature than himself; frightened men who knew that it was his head, or theirs.

ii

Had we been alive and in Paris one evening in June 1794 standing in the rue St. Honoré opposite No. 366, we should have seen a slightly built man, erect and with an air of superiority about him, walk down the street from the rue Royale and turn into the courtyard of the Maison Duplay.

He was dressed for a great occasion—white breeches, light blue coat, broad tricolour sash, and plumes of the same colours in his hat. We should certainly have recognised him, for he was the President of the National Convention returning from his greatest triumph, the

Feast of the Supreme Being, dedicated on the Champ de Mars to the God of his own creation.

Inside the little house there was excitement and happiness, for a son had been born that day to Elisabeth, one of the Duplay sisters, and now married to Robespierre's friend Philippe Lebas. The Duplay family living at No. 366 consisted of Maurice the father, his wife, three sisters, Eléonore, Elisabeth, and Victoire, Duplay's son Jacques and his nephew Simon. All vied with one another to give the dictator the home they felt he ought to have; he was surrounded by attention, his wants anticipated, his wishes instantly obeyed; and to the salon beyond the dining room came most of the great men of the Revolution during the time that Robespierre lived in the house.

There can be no doubt that in the little bed-sitting-room on the first floor which he occupied he composed those long and often tedious orations by which the Convention was first enthralled and then exasperated, and in which the insistent theme was always *Virtue*, *Virtue* in the individual and *Virtue* in the nation. How the Convention came to hate that word!

It was in that same room that he sat down to write the last speech he was to make, his defence against the charges that he had become a dictator, that he had conspired against liberty. Dictator he certainly had been up to that day, June 8, when he had presided over the Feast of the Supreme Being, while of liberty there was clearly none after June 10, when he signed the Law of Prairial. But he was confident that the Convention would listen to him as it always had done, and he seems to have had no intuition that the end was near.

He spent the sixth and seventh Thermidor (July) writing and rewriting his speech in his minute, orderly hand. Until he had finished he only left the house once, for a stroll with Eléonore who loved him and who, though they were never betrothed, wore mourning for him till she died, still unmarried, nearly fifty years later. With him on that quiet walk he took his dog, Brount, of whom he was very fond, and who slept always in the room with him.

He read his speech in the Convention on the eighth, and though it was heard to the end, it was coldly received. He had made accusations without mentioning names, with the inevitable result that many who heard him felt their necks stiffen with the thought of the guillotine, and murmured: "It is now or never, him or me." In the evening he re-read his speech to the Jacobins, where he had a hysterical success, and went home to the Maison Duplay in mixed and chastened mood. At the end of his speech, he had told the Jacobins that he was ready to die; "to drink the hemlock," he said.

That night at No. 366, and the calm sleep into which he fell, were the last he was to know in the house of his friends. Next day, the ninth, he dressed in his brilliant blue coat, spoke a few words to the anxious family, and went through the little wooden door into the quiet courtyard which we can see today, and so, via the rue St. Honoré, to the National Convention in the Tuileries.

The story of that tempestuous afternoon and the terrible night and day that followed cannot be compressed into a few sentences. It deserves, indeed demands, to be read in full in any of the great histories of the period. Only here, for those who are still curious, can be sketched in briefest outline the tremendous drama in which Robespierre perished, and with him the Terror which he had created.

In the Convention all went awry for him from the beginning. They shouted his friend St. Just off the tribune, refusing to hear his cold recital of facts concerning the inner history of the Committee of Public Safety; and that extraordinary man made no further attempt to have his say, though he knew well enough that unless he did, this day would be his last. Robespierre's enemies—Tallien, Collot d'Herbois, Thuriot and Legendre (friends of Danton, executed three months earlier at Robespierre's command) Billaud-Varenne, an old opponent,—all these, and more, attacked him one after the other, each launching out in increasing tirade against the personal dictatorship of one man, and that man Robespierre. Maximilien tried to speak, was shouted down, raised his high-pitched voice to scream at the chairman, calling him "President of Assassins!" and remained standing and gesticulating, his self-control gone, while round him the roar of "Traitor!" grew and would not be silenced. Finally he was arrested with his friends, and after darkness had fallen they were taken separately to various prisons in the city.

But it was not to end as easily as that. By devious means, and because the gaolers could not believe that Robespierre was really a prisoner, they were rescued by their friends of the Commune, the municipal authority of Paris, and in the Hotel de Ville [destroyed in 1871] they gathered to play their last desperate card—the calling out of the "sections," the working people of Paris, to march against the Convention. A revolution was to be made against the Revolution.

Today you may see in the Carnavalet Museum, 23 rue de Sévigné, the written call to arms made by these desperate men on the threshold of catastrophe. Low down on the right hand side are the letters "*Ro.*" All through the evening the others had tried to persuade Robespierre to sign and he had refused. He was still the lawyer, and his pedantry, his bigotry, never showed more clearly than in this refusal to sign the order because, he argued, it was not legal. At last he took up the pen, but having written the first two letters of his name, stopped and would not complete it. Outside, the bells of St. Germain—l'Auxerrois half a mile away—which sounded in 1572 for the massacre of the Huguenots—were ringing the tocsin, calling the citizens to arms against the fallen dictator.

While the others were arguing and pleading with him, the men of the Convention, armed, burst into the Hotel de Ville and the room in which the conspirators were sitting. A young man named Méda shot Robespierre as he sat at the table, the bullet breaking the left side of his jaw, and he sealed with his blood the paper on which he would not write his name. The dark brown stains on the parchment bear witness to it to this day.

Lebas shot himself when he saw the soldiers on the steps outside the building; Augustin Robespierre hurled himself from the roof to the street below, survived and was captured; Couthon the cripple hid, was found and wounded; St. Just remained with Maximilien and made no move, spoke no word. They were taken to the Convention, and in the Tuileries Robespierre lay for hours, bleeding and half-conscious on a table, while his enemies gazed at him and lesser men mocked him. The table is today in the Hotel de Soubise (Archives Nationales) No. 60, rue des Francs-Bourgeois, off the rue Vieille du Temple.

From there, they were sent to the Conciergerie to be made ready for the guillotine.

iii

Had we been alive and in Paris that evening, July 28, 1794, standing in the rue St. Honoré opposite No. 366, we should have been among thousands who crowded the route to see the Terror go by. Every window above and on either side of us was crammed with excited people; but not the windows opposite. Behind the shutters of No. 366 two women were alone, weeping and praying. One was Eléonore, the other Elisabeth, widowed when Lebas shot himself the night before. Duplay and his wife were already in prison, the man to survive, the woman to die there.

Had we remained in the crowded street, we should have seen, after a long wait, the carts approach and stop opposite for a brief and terrible moment while guttersnipes defiled the doorway of the house that had been

Robespierre's home. We should have seen the man himself, half-dead already, his jaws held together by a dirty cloth, his hands bound behind his back, pass on in the jolting tumbril till it reached the corner of the rue Royale. There we should have seen it turn, and slowly pass from sight.

Had we stayed a little longer, we should have heard from the mass of people by the scaffold the sound of wild, continued cheering. And we should have known that he was dead.

iv

Of all the Revolutionary pilgrimages open to the curious, that to the Maison Duplay is the easiest to make. In the first place, part of the house exists and it is in the heart of the tourists' Paris. Everyone who has found himself in Paris more than once in his life knows the rue St. Honoré; moreover, the pilgrim needs no car, and no more physical energy than is necessary to carry him a few hundred yards from the corner of the rue Royale eastwards down the St. Honoré, to find on its northern side No. 398-400. On the right is a ladies' hairdressing salon, on the left a *pâtisserie* with a bakery behind. Between the two is the entrance.

The first time, many years ago, that I ventured to penetrate the forbidding passage between the street and the little courtyard beyond, I felt apprehensive, uneasy. I did not know what to expect, what to look for, and seeing an old woman playing a broom on some steps as I emerged from the passage, I hesitated. As usual, curiosity got the better of me, and I asked the woman if she could tell me, where was the Maison Duplay?

"*La porte de Robespierre, monsieur*," she answered unemotionally, and with a wave of the broom-stick towards the other end of the yard, added "*C'est là*." And went on with her sweeping. Evidently I was no trespasser, and no curiosity either.

I looked around. The court is narrow, running at right angles to the street outside. The first thing to catch the eye is a flight of three steps leading to the doorway on the left hand side, those which were being swept as

Porte de Robespierre in the courtyard of the Maison Duplay

I entered. The building to which this door gives entrance has today six storeys, of which only the ground and first floors hold an interest for us. This is the main part of the Duplay house, and in the building next to it, now joined as one, but then detached, Robespierre had his room on the first floor. Facing us, at right angles to the other, is a further building, and it is in the corner where the two meet that the door of Robespierre stands.

When I first saw it, it was painted a dark green, almost black; cobwebs hung unbroken over its two large panels and over the grille at the top. It looked what it was—old, neglected, but important, and from it exuded that strange oppressiveness which haunts the places of the past. It is small, it hides itself away in this corner, it belongs to a great epoch, yet it is marked by no plaque or monument. ["The door of Robespierre" is protected by the Municipality of Paris; in July 1957 it had been cleaned and re-painted grey. It is proposed at some future date to place a memorial plaque on the entrance to the passage, in the rue St. Honoré.] Only a few yards away the noise of modern Paris comes strangely through the passage, halts confused, and eddies weakly back from whence it came.

I stood for a long time in front of this door, thinking of its story, of what it had seen and heard in all its lengthening years. For this is the door which Maurice Duplay the cabinet maker had specially installed when Robespierre rose to greatness under his roof. It gave a separate guarded entrance to a new stairway which led up to his bedroom. It was fitted, in those days, with a massive lock, and bolts on the inner side. Behind it, I thought, lies history. Timidly I touched it, ran my finger along the bottom of the lower panel, felt the dust move with my finger, thought of Thermidor, and shivered.

The woman had stopped sweeping, and I heard her clattering somewhere inside the other doorway. I came back into the courtyard and looked up at the first floor windows. At that time I had not seen the plans in Lenôtre's *Paris Révolutionnaire*, so each meant as much to me as its neighbour. Only I knew it was on the first floor that Robespierre had lived. After a little while I went away, planning to return and enter the house itself if I could, for I was determined to see behind the door.

It was some years before I turned again into the dark passage, through into the courtyard and stood in front of it. This time no one was about, the place was silent. Nothing was changed, and I was no better informed about it than I had been. Bolder this time, I went up the stone steps, and tried the handle of the other door, the one nearest the street. Locked. Had I seen anyone I might have asked for leave to enter. I say might, because you have to be determined with yourself about these things—I have always the feeling that I am an intruder. In any case, I left without my question put, for there was no one to put it to.

During the war years, when Paris was ruled by the Nazis, I never read a newspaper report of life in the city, or of some event there, without thinking about the Maison Duplay and its courtyard. When I heard that Paris had been bombed, that street fighting had broken out between men of the Resistance and the Germans, I became anxious lest after all these years violence should touch the old house from which so much violence had once emerged. After the capital had been liberated, it was with relief that I heard from friends that the only visible signs of war in the centre of Paris were on the face of the Crillon Hotel in the Place de la Concorde, and a block of houses destroyed by German bombs in the closing days of the battle for the city.

It was more than a year later when I returned, this time with fortune at my side, for I was able to enter the old house at last.

V

As I walked along the now familiar passage I could sense the change, and the moment I came into the courtyard, there it was in front of me: nothing less than a smart Parisian bar! Where a plain wall had been there now appeared a front of polished wood and smooth plate glass. Shining lights and sounds of voices met my astonished sight and hearing, and I stood blinking like a disappointed child staring at a shop window from which a coveted toy has been removed.

Recovering myself, I looked to see if the rest of the house still stood, half prepared to find it gone as well. No, there were the three stone steps, the first door with the stairs behind it, and the quiet windows on the first floor. Something saved, I thought, but what about the wooden door? I walked quickly to see, and there it was still in its dark corner, but it had changed. Where before it had glimmered in its ancient green or black, now it shone in a bright new coat of cream and white. My first thought was of annoyance, for the thing looked wrong. Who had laid such hands upon it? Did they not know its history? Then, thinking again, it seemed unreasonable to deny it the paint without which it must finally decay. As I stood there undecided, another door opened in the polished wood at my side, and a waiter in a white coat smilingly asked me to enter.

I walked in without a word, as though I was dreaming. All this brightness of light and sharpness of sound about me seemed a phantasy. For years I had read about this house, steeped myself in its atmosphere, visited it in awe, and hoped one day to enter, hat in hand, on tip-toe. And now, here I was in the dining room of the Duplay family —and the ghosts were drinking dry martinis. From further back in the room came the sounds of a sad jazz-band moaning from a loud-speaker on the wall.

I sank on to a high stool before the bar and ordered a large whisky and soda. When I had recovered, I asked the barman if he knew where he was working. He smiled.

"Yes, monsieur. *Chez Robespierre,*" he replied. Then, seeing *Paris Révolutionnaire* lying by my hat, he asked if I would like to see the *patron,* and in a few moments the *patron* and I were drinking each other's health while he told me of his new venture, and I of the errand that had brought me there.

He was interested, sympathetic, and intelligent. He knew something, though not all, of the story of the Maison Duplay, and showed me the little verse he had printed on the cover of his menu cards, inviting his guests to remember in a toast the man of the Revolution. He was not, he said, the owner of the house. I asked who was, and when he said, "she" could be found next door, I suggested he should introduce me to her then and there, to which he gladly agreed. He led me into the courtyard, and together we went through the passage into the busy street. I was still walking on air, and had the delicious feeling that anything could happen.

In the *pâtisserie* my new friend led me past the counter to the back of the shop, where fresh new loaves smelling of the bakery were coming in from a doorway futher on. He spoke to one of the men, and a few minutes later I was face to face with the owner of the Maison Duplay.

Madame Chambolle greeted me with charm. Yes, she knew of course that this was Robespierre's house, but had made no study of it. I offered her my Lenôtre, and as she read one or two of the pages, her eyes grew bright with interest, and in quick colloquial French she remarked to the *patron* that this and that was still unaltered. She was clearly enjoying it, and soon she made the suggestion I had been hoping for. "Would monsieur like to see over the house?"

"Madame," I said, "I have been waiting many years for this moment."

"Well then, let us go."

She called for her keys and led the way through the doorway at the back. I followed, the *patron* behind me. First we came into a narrow passage, opening into a small room of beautiful proportions in which was stored the flour for the bakery. All was still exactly as Lenôtre had found it in 1894, when he had come on this same pilgrimage. I could not resist reading aloud the moving words in which he has recaptured for all time the picture of this salon when it held these fiery men, as they talked, sang, argued, plotted. Here, between these walls and on this very floor!

We stood silent for a time, and I felt close to the core of things, seeing not the white flour piled against the walls, but the shape and form of lives lived long ago.

We went down into the cool basement, and I could hear the sound of the bakers as they walked along the passage above. So, I thought, may the two girls, Eléonore and Elisabeth, in the fearful days that followed Thermidor, have heard the footsteps of the police coming to seal up Robespierre's room, as they cowered there alone. I was glad when we came up into the light.

"And what of the floor above, madame?" I asked.

"It is an office, monsieur. I will show it to you. You shall see it all."

We made our way back to the courtyard, this time to go up the stone steps and through the door which I had found locked before the war. I followed madame up the stairs, those stairs which had led to the bedrooms of the Duplays. At the top, off a small landing, we entered some offices, where the friendly manager of the company making cosmetics showed me the upper rooms of the old house.

With Lenôtre's plan in my hand it was not difficult to trace, by the shape of the walls, where the lawyer from Arras had lived, slept, and written from 1791 to 1794; easy, too, to plot the room of the Duplays, father and mother, and lastly the bedroom of their daughters, with the window looking out on to the little garden. Now, as when Lenôtre saw it, this is covered over by a glass roof, but today the garden has become part of the tea-room. You eat ice-cream where the flowers grew.

Here I read to them again, this time the page in which the patient master of research sets down his own sad thoughts as he stood here fifty years ago, in contemplation of the joys and the sorrows, the hopes and the agonies, this quiet room had known. When I stopped reading, I found myself looking at one of the young typists. She was sitting near the end of the room, her machine in front of her. Cupboards filled with letters and files stood against the wall where once the dresses of Eléonore Duplay had hung. The girl had stopped her typing when I entered the room, and now she sat quiet, full of her own thoughts.

Before I said goodbye to Madame Chambolle, I asked her to write her name on one of Lenôtre's pages; it would mark the day for me, I said, and to myself I thought: "It will prove I am not dreaming."

After she had gone, the *patron* and I sat down at the bar once more and I told him how I had always wanted to see behind the door of Robespierre. He got down from the stool, beckoning me to follow him, and I saw that he was smiling. He stopped in front of a built-in cupboard in a corner of the bar and opened it.

"Look," he said. I peered into the gloom. A light switched on above. In front of me was a wash basin, and behind the door of Robespierre was nothing more terrible than a roller-towel, damp and rather frayed at the edges.

vi

Again, recently, I visited No. 398. A friend was with me, who had said he would like to see the courtyard of the Maison Duplay.

It was a Sunday, and at eleven o'clock in the morning there were few people in the rue St. Honoré. As we entered the courtyard our footsteps rang out sharply. The door above the steps was locked firmly. It was very warm and close in the little yard, and above it the windows of the Duplays were shut and bolted.

We stood in front of Robespierre's door while I told my friend a little of its story, and as we talked a dog began to howl somewhere in the building. At first we paid no heed to it, until it grew and drowned our voices. We listened, looking up at the Maison Duplay.

Soon the whole courtyard was filled with the sorrowful baying, and I remembered that on his last evening's walk with Eléonore, three days before he died, Robespierre had taken with him his dog Brount, of whom he was very fond, and who slept always in his room.

Concerning the Maison Duplay, it is right to point out that there is a conflict of opinion among the experts, not indeed about its site, but about the house itself as we see it today and as it has remained since the early days of the nineteenth century.

Lenôtre in 1894 was satisfied, after a searching analysis of the title-deeds and documents of the house, that when in 1811 and 1816 the upper storeys were added, the old part—the ground and the first floors—was left more or less intact. Ralph Korngold is of the same opinion (*Robespierre, the First Modern Dictator*, Macmillan, 1937, p. 120). Hilaire Belloc, writing in 1901 (*Robespierre, a Study*, James Nisbet & Co. Ltd., pp. 375-76) is equally certain that this is not so, and quotes the architect's report when the additions were being made in which he advises that the walls and foundations of the old house were not strong enough to bear the extra load of four more storeys. Belloc agrees, however, that the rooms on the ground and first floors were reproduced roughly to the same plan, and correspond in width and height to the original. Both Lenôtre and Belloc confirm that the courtyard is the same, with one building added on the right hand side which does not concern us.

Choose which you will, you can see for yourself that the door is there, the courtyard is there; the touch of history remains, vibrant, strong as ever.

Maillard, organizer of the massacres at the Carmelite convent

9. HERE THEY FELL

The September Massacres

i

The Tuileries, ancient palace of the French monarchy on the north bank of the Seine, was conceived by Catherine de Medici in the mid-sixteenth century and various French kings added to it. The two wings stand today (the northern much rebuilt), but Catherine's central block, after two sackings by Parisian mobs, with one of which we are concerned, was finally destroyed by fire during the Commune riots in 1871 and its ruins pulled down two years later.

If you walk south towards the river from the golden statue of Joan of Arc in the rue de Rivoli (Place des

Pyramides) along the short Avenue Paul Déroulède you will pass on your left the wide empty space where the palace stood, between the pavilions of Marsan and Flore. Here later Napoleon lived with Josephine, and later still his nephew, Napoleon III, with Eugénie.

In front of it, and little changed, are the famous Tuileries Gardens, created in the latter half of the seventeenth century for Louis XIV by Le Notre, designer also of the gardens at Versailles, and one of the greatest garden architects of all time. The gardens played a vital part in the story.

The assault on the Tuileries by armed mobs on the morning of August 10, 1792, was the turning point of the Revolution. In two terrible hours, while the Palace became a slaughter house for a thousand Swiss guards, the French Monarchy ceased to exist. France had taken the plunge, throwing aside the rule of a fumbling Parliament and a discredited but still legally responsible King, for a Republic born with fear in its heart and violence in its hands. For three days the King and Queen and their children remained in the sweltering Parliament building, watching their new masters through a little window; then the mists of the Temple swallowed them up, and nothing was ever the same again.

France and her revolution had reached that point of desperate balance which all upheavals reach sooner or later—they had to conquer or die. The Prussian armies were across her borders, the new French armies were in full retreat before them, the Eastern fortresses invested and about to surrender. Panic seized the people, and with panic came terror. Rumour flew before the dissolving

French soldiers and the people believed their last hours had come.

In such conditions, every aristocrat, every royalist, every priest who refused to swear the new oath to the Republic became in the people's eyes a traitor, and the police, urged on by the Paris Commune, in wild unreason swept them into prisons or herded them into filthy dungeons all over Paris—men, women and children without distinction. As the news of the disasters at Longwy and Verdun poured in, only the wisest and the bravest resisted the mass impulse to destroy these wretched hostages while there was yet time. To be a prisoner in Paris in those last weeks of August was to be on the brink of violent death.

Everywhere the people rushed to volunteer, crying, "Let us fight. Give us arms and we will fight and win! But before we go, let us kill these monsters in the prisons, or they will break out in our absence and murder our wives and children. Give us swords and pikes and axes and let us settle with our enemies here, and then we will settle with them out there." So, while the shivering wretches in the prisons waited paralysed with apprehension, the avenging eyes of the people turned in their direction.

On the morning of September 2, the rumour spread through the excited streets that a great plot had been discovered. It went from house to house and street to street that the traitors in the prisons were going to break out and join the hordes of royalists, hidden in the city, in a mass attack on the people. "To the prisons then! Let us finish it!" Soon the mobs were on the move to

La Force, l'Abbaye, Bicêtre, and all the other rat-infested holes where the priests and aristocrats waited, their livid faces pressed against the windows, or on their knees asking for courage and a quick end.

So began the September massacres, which literally drenched with blood the courtyards of the prisons and the streets outside them. Men and women became primaeval savages as they hacked and bludgeoned all that day and half the night. Many terrible things were done. There were some who died crying for mercy, some who shouted "Long live the King," some who lied and were spared, some who told the truth and perished. But for the most part they died without a word, over two thousand of them, the old with the young, the weak with the strong. When morning came the drunken hordes staggered away to their hovels, covered with blood, wearing the jewellery and the clothes stripped from their victims.

Then, with one fear removed from their minds, the men went out in their thousands to join the armies, to fight for liberty, equality, fraternity, to save their young Republic from the enemy now approaching their very doorstep.

ii

The prisons of revolutionary Paris have either disappeared, or like the Conciergerie are so changed as to be only museums and show places for the curious. There is one old house, however, where the tide of murder swept in on September 2, which has survived intact—the Convent of the Carmelites. It stands in the rue de Vaugirard, south of the river, and is today a religious college.

Because of the stark horror that its walls have seen, and of the fact that practically nothing of the building has been changed, it is one of the most extraordinary revolutionary relics in Paris. Below ground level in the cool vaults of the chapel are gathered together the shattered skulls and naked bones of between seventy and eighty out of a hundred and twenty people, mostly priests, who were murdered there. They are wedged tightly into great glass cases, the electric light throwing them into gleaming contrast with the velvet cloth on which they rest, and you stand before them in a kind of stupor. So many skulls, so many bones, rows and rows of them, produce on you at length a cold feeling of guilt which grows intolerable. The eyeless sockets and the grinning teeth are too close, too real; you feel in panic that the grisly things which once were men will of a sudden disentangle, skulls rattle on to spines, legs and thighs and arms fly to their proper places, and shattering the thin glass sheet which pens them in sweep over you to find once more the lives they lost in swift tragedy on the garden steps above.

The chapel crypt, as I say, is open to the public, but

the house itself is not, except by special permission. I was fortunate enough to have received an invitation from the Abbé in charge of the college to visit it, and with him as my guide to have the privilege, accorded to few foreigners, of going through the corridors and rooms of this old house, now so peaceful with its quiet students, then so filled with shouting and so soiled with crime.

iii

Even an accomplished Parisian like Monsieur Krok was puzzled when I asked him to drive me to the *Couvent des Carmes*. Yes, he had heard of it, he said, but it took a few minutes, searching on the map before we located it in the rue de Vaugirard. It was on the right hand side of the road as we drove westwards, and we pulled up opposite the entrance to the chapel, with its graceful tower and dome. I told him to wait on the other side of the road, in the shade.

On the wall of the chapel courtyard is a notice giving the hours and days when the crypt is open; today was one of them, and already a little knot of people stood waiting to go in. I was a little early for my appointment with the Abbé, so I joined them and listened to their conversation.

There was a little family of three, the father a jolly, middle-aged man with bald head and ample stomach —a small shopkeeper perhaps—his stolid wife, wearing her simple black dress with a touch of grace, and holding by the hand a girl of ten or so, dark like her father. Next to them an old man stood leaning on a stick, gazing intently through the railings as though expecting a friend or relative to appear in the courtyard and greet him by name. He was tall and well-dressed, with a soft black hat: a retired lawyer or doctor with a bent for history perhaps. Behind him a young couple waited, talking in low tones and consulting a book from time to time. The boy—nineteen or so—had the keen intelligent face of the Latin. The girl with him was short and very trim in a white blouse and pale yellow skirt. She had the sort of teeth a film star would envy, and her blue eyes were more often on the boy than the book he held for her to read. The little group was completed by a workman in blue over-alls and a beret worn over his eyes. He was smoking a cigarette and reading a sporting newspaper. A few minutes after I joined them, two Zouaves sauntered along the pavement, caught sight of the notice painted on the wall, and after reading it and asking the man in overalls what it was all about, decided to join us.

So there we were, ten odd people on one of the hottest days in Paris for years, all waiting for the ancient gate of the Carmelites to open and let us in—that same gate, and those same railings, through which the murderers from the Faubourg St. Antoine had burst to massacre the prisoners inside the chapel in September, 1792.

As the bell in the convent chimed the hour, a woman came clattering along the cloister with a string of keys in her hand, and seeing her the little group moved towards the gate, the girl of ten holding tightly to her mother. With a rusty rattle the woman on the other side of the railings unlocked the gate, and it creaked as though it had remained shut for a long time. We filed into the courtyard and waited while the gate was locked behind us. Again I had the queer sensation which all these old revolutionary places give me, of slipping back through the years.

The stones of the courtyard, the grey chapel facing us, the dim and echoing cloister down which we walked, are unchanged these 150 years. Only the sudden hooting of a lorry in the rue de Vaugirard assaulted the heavy atmosphere.

I had been so interested in watching my companions that I had forgotten my appointment with the Abbé, and now hastened to ask the woman with the keys where he should be found. "*Monsieur l'Abbé?*" She stopped and looked at me with curious eyes. "He is not here, monsieur," she said, and turning, hurried on through a door in the archway ahead of us, followed closely by the other visitors, who obviously resented my unexpected interruption. I was in a quandary. The Abbé was no doubt waiting for me (I was already ten minutes late) and clearly I should get no help from the woman. I turned to go back, then remembered that the gate was locked.

How silly of me, I thought, to get into such a muddle. There was nothing for it but to follow on and hope to find my way inside, so I hurried after the others, as the Zouaves, last in the party, disappeared through the archway in the shadows.

There must be, as Lenôtre has said, a special dispensation for those who, however unimportant, follow the will-o-the-wisp of historical research, for just as I was going through the archway I heard someone come out of a door and down some stone steps on the other side of the cloister. I turned to look, and saw a young man, almost a boy, in the black gown of a priest about to cross the open courtyard.

"Pardon me, monsieur," I said. "I am looking for the Abbé, who is expecting me. Could you take me to him, please?"

He stopped, and answered kindly, "Certainly, monsieur. But you are in the wrong part of the building. Monsieur l'Abbé lives in the college, in the rue d'Assas. Follow me, please," and with that he set off with a swinging stride, back to the gate through which we had entered from the street. He opened it for me, and then, with his hand on the gate, he said:

"Go down the street, monsieur, until you come to the rue d'Assas—there," and he pointed to where it crossed the rue de Vaugirard about fifty yards away. "Turn to your right, and a few yards down you will see the entrance to the college on your right. Go through the covered courtyard, and ask the Concierge inside for the Abbé."

I thanked him for his kindness and with a smile and a bow he re-locked the gate, walked back across the courtyard and disappeared into the cloister.

I hurried off down the street as he had directed me, and soon I was asking the Concierge inside the college to show me the way to the house of the Abbé. The man came out of his little room and walked a few yards with me till we came into the open on a wide path running on all sides of the convent except the east, where a high wall separates it from the road outside. The chapel and the courtyard where I had first entered were now over on my right hand side, the convent, in front of which I now stood, lying to the northeast of the chapel. The Concierge left me at the inner entrance to the college, and I went through an archway and up the stone stairs. On the landing above was a door with a gilt knocker, which I used to announce my belated arrival. A pleasant voice said "*Entrez,*" and I pushed open the door.

iv

A tall middle-aged man rose from his chair to greet me. His face, dominated by eyes which were clear and penetrating, gave me at once a feeling of confidence. His handshake was firm, his voice deep and colourful, and his natural dignity perfectly suited the black vestment he wore. He seemed pleased to see me, and when I was seated opposite him with a small table between us, he asked me what I would like to do.

I told him the reason for my being in Paris, and in his house, of my long interest in everything concerning the Revolution, and that I had read about the massacre in the Convent of the Carmelites, some account of which I hoped to include in the book I was writing in my spare time. He raised his eyebrows at this and said: "But you are a historian, are you not, monsieur?"

"No, Monsieur l'Abbé," I replied, "I am not. I am a railwayman whose hobby has been for many years to go about Paris trying to re-discover the streets, houses and buildings in which men and women of the Revolution lived or died, and seeing what these places are like today."

He smiled.

"I am honoured, monsieur, to receive you here. I am afraid that in France, and indeed in the world today, many of us are too absorbed in the life of the moment to spare much time to think of the past. This old house has seen many things, and I will gladly show it to you."

But first he told me something of its history. It was built by the Carmelite friars in 1620, with the chapel, and the work they did for the poor of the neighbourhood ensured them the respect and affection of the people. Here they lived and worked unhindered, and they were here still in 1792 when the September massacres took place. The popular fury was not directed against the friars, but against the priests and the royalists, and when the mob heard that there were over a hundred priests in the convent and the chapel, they determined to break in and kill them. The friars were powerless to resist, though Lenôtre says they did what they could to comfort the victims waiting to go before the self-appointed judge for their mockery of a trial.

As the Abbé talked, I looked round the room in which we sat. There were books on the shelves, the furniture was simple, and this man had impressed his quiet personality upon the place. I could have sat listening to him, and was hoping he would continue to talk, when he got up, and walking to the door said to me:

"I must not weary you, monsieur. It is the house that is important, and not my words. Will you follow me, if you please? We will go first to the chapel, where the priests were herded together, and then I will show you how it happened, taking the route they took, so that you may have it clearly in your mind."

He held the door open for me and we went downstairs together, out onto the pathway and through some open-air passages to a door in the side of the chapel, which he unlocked. He motioned me to go in first. The chapel is no larger than the average village church in England, but, as one would expect, more ornate and a good deal loftier. After pointing out a number of religious paintings, the Abbé took me by the arm and led me to a little aisle on the left hand side.

"Here they stood, monsieur," he told me, "waiting for hours, expecting to be honourably tried and acquitted, for they knew they had committed no crime of any kind. They went through that door one by one at short intervals. Now, please, be good enough to follow me again."

We left the chapel, and I found myself in a large pleasant room with long tables by the walls, and a spotless wooden floor.

"They came through here," he said, "on their way to the little place I shall show you next." I followed him through a door on the far side. Now we stood at the foot of a staircase, and in front a passage led to the garden which I could see at the far end through an open door. Slightly to the left, half under the staircase, was a sort of recess, rather dark and just big enough for a man to sit at a table. The Abbé stopped, and stood in the recess.

"It was here, monsieur, that Maillard set up the judge's table," he said.

"You mean they were tried, here, in this corridor?"

"In a way they were tried, yes, monsieur; but it was of course a mockery, a sham. They were all marked for death, it was simply a cruel and useless formality. The so-called judge, surrounded by others like him, put some questions to each victim as he came before him from the other room." I pictured the scene. . . .

"Your name, citizen?"

"So and so."

"You are a priest and you have refused to take the oath to the Republic?"

"My oath is to God. I have committed no crime. I hope to be acquitted and set at liberty."

"We shall see about that, citizen. If you are a good man, you have nothing to fear."

The bloodshot eyes look up sarcastically, the men around him laugh.

"You must go from here, citizen, to stand your trial."

That was all, the same enigmatic remark to each one. . . .

The Abbé was talking again.

"As the judge spoke the words 'to stand your trial,' the victim was hurried down this passage." He turned and walked towards the garden outside. I followed, and when we came into the open we found ourselves on a little stone platform, from which three or four steps led down to the path on either side. An iron railing stood on the garden side of the platform. The Abbé was silent for a moment, his eyes looking out over the garden in the bright sunshine. Then he turned to me and said quietly:

"You stand now, monsieur, on one of the sacred places of the Revolution."

I had read the story. As each man came out onto this little landing, he saw the assassins waiting for him on the steps. He was seized from one side or the other, and immediately cut down, to fall bleeding among his murderers. If he was not already dead he was dragged onto the path below and bludgeoned, stabbed or shot, and his body flung on to the growing heap of corpses in the garden. A few, the younger and more vigorous, leaped the railing and ran into the garden, where they were caught and butchered like the rest, except for two or three who managed to reach the wall at the end and miraculously scaled it to safety. Neither the Abbé nor I said a word as we stood there. I was grateful to him for his silence.

Then we walked down the steps on which a hundred and twenty men had died, and into the garden. We sat down on a seat and he told me about the college of which he was the head. The pupils studying for the priesthood live in the cool dormitories which stretch on both sides of the passages on every floor. Their day is very full, he said, and they acquire much happiness during the time they spend at the Carmelites. There is of course no luxury, but they have simple comforts, and the priests I saw walking about the garden looked hard and strong.

It was refreshing to spend an hour in their company, and I envied their grace and poise. These young men, I thought, are going soon to the towns and villages of France, to live among the people, to comfort them, to lose themselves in life-long service to their fellowmen. They will look back from time to time, and draw renewed hope and faith from this old house and garden, and from the wise man who sat beside me.

While we talked, an elderly priest came down the path, and the Abbé rose to greet him. They conversed together for a few minutes; the older man was putting some problem to the Abbé, who listened quietly and spoke now and then with certainty, and finally with decision. The other smiled, they gave each other a little bow, then the priest retraced his steps and disappeared into the building. They had stood just out of earshot, but by their gestures and their faces I could follow the trend of it. This little world set in the midst of Paris seemed to me very complete, very satisfying.

I got up from the seat as the Abbé turned to me again.

"If you have a few minutes more," he said, "there are some things in the convent that will interest you."

We walked back by a different path, and in at another door; from here we made our way through various small rooms to a solid-looking door which, when unlocked, revealed a narrow descending corridor. The Abbé went first, and at the end of the passage, through another door, we came into the crypt with its stacked skulls and bones.

On September 3, 1792, when the madness had passed, the bodies were gathered together and given a hasty common burial in an old well in the middle of the garden. Years later, the then owner of the property, Mme. de Soyécourt, ordered the grave to be reopened. She had bought the convent and chapel from the government in memory of her father, a victim of the guillotine. There was difficulty in locating it, and it is said that an old man who refused to give his name pointed out the correct site to the labourers. With the bones they found a quantity of clothes, jewellery and ornaments, plates and cups and meat bones—the remains of a meal taken by those who had buried the bodies. From this well the bones were taken to the crypt at Mme. de Soyécourt's wish, to rest there in holy ground.

As I recrossed the room leading from the chapel to the outer cloister, I saw the little party of pilgrims with whom I first entered the place. They were standing in the courtyard looking up at the chapel tower. The woman with the keys was already letting in another batch from the street outside. The family of three was standing a little apart from the others. The little girl was not looking at the chapel, but had turned round and seemed absorbed in the traffic passing in the rue de Vaugirard. She still held her mother's hand, but languidly. To her young mind this place meant little; she was looking forward, the special privilege of youth. The man I took to be a doctor was pointing out something with his stick to the girl with the yellow skirt, whose companion was still consulting his book. The workman had taken off his beret and rolled up his sporting newspaper; he was talking to the two Zouaves, and they were engaged in an argument, for they were all talking and the Zouaves were emphasizing their words with their arms. A discussion on the Rights of Man, and the still unsolved problems of Rousseau's Ideal State, was not, I felt, out of place in such surroundings.

Then the Abbé led me upstairs, and in a small room he showed me the place where the madmen had stacked their swords and axes. Down the wall the blood of the martyrs had dripped from the weapons which had killed them. It is still there, a faint but terrible witness, preserved for all time from the atmosphere by a glass casing which stands in front of it.

I have seen all or nearly all that there is left to see in Paris which speaks to us of that great upward thrust of man to greater freedom and dignity which we call the French Revolution, and what there is of horror too.

Dungeons that have held the mighty and the famous, the unknown and the lowly, thick doors and bolts which cut off life and love and the world outside, the table on which a dictator lived his last hours stretched in agony, letters too intimate, too shattering in their courage and their devotion for long inspection, gloves and shoes, shirts and napkins, and a Queen's scent in a stoppered bottle exactly as she left it; but these pale red lines of what had been alive and warm are different and apart. They are stark, they bring history close, they intensify the mystery of living and dying.

They ask a terrible question: How long is it since we were savages?

V

I said goodbye to the Abbé outside his room, and thanked him for the honour he had done me, a foreigner, by allowing me to enter this historic place. As I left the building, something made me turn again to the garden. I walked along the path among the flowering shrubs and through the trees that line it on either side. Under one of these I found a little stone set in a piece of brickwork, with a faded inscription on it which I could not read. It marks the place where they killed one of the priests who had escaped death on the steps. On my way back I noticed for the first time a stone on the face of the steps just below the iron railing where the priests had died. Two words only were cut into it: "*Hic Ceciderunt.*" ("Here they fell.")

When I regained the rue d'Assas, I was still thinking of that dark recess where Maillard, the organiser of massacre, had set up his judge's table, and of the little window above, through which from time to time he had watched the killing going on below. I must have turned to the right instead of the left, for I wandered on towards the river, and stood for a long while leaning on the stone parapet watching the slow Seine flowing by. Then I crossed over the Pont du Carrousel into the Tuileries gardens, and so back to my hotel, before I remembered that Monsieur Krok (no doubt asleep by now) was still waiting for me in the rue de Vaugirard.

10. THE END OF ROYALTY

The Temple Prison

i

Sometime after eight o'clock on the morning of August 10, 1792, a small party of people, with two children, came through the main doors of the Tuileries Palace on the west side, went down the broad steps and walked slowly through the formal gardens in the direction of the Place Louis XV, now Place de la Concorde and, during the Terror, Place de la Révolution. About half way between the Palace and the Square, the little party turned to the right, and finally left the gardens by some steps, to disappear into the long Riding School which was being used by the Assembly as the Parlement building. (If you stand today where the rue de Castiglione joins the rue de Rivoli the steps are exactly opposite.)

The portly, clumsy figure at their head was Louis XVI, King of France, and the little boy who held his hand as he went along the path was the Dauphin; behind father and son came the Queen, Marie-Antoinette, her face flushed with anger, her head high in defiance; with her was her young daughter, Madame Royale, Mme. Elisabeth, the King's sister, and two ladies of the Court, the Princesse de Lamballe, the Queen's friend, and the Duchesse de Tourzel, the devoted governess of the royal children, who left her own young daughter in the Palace rather than desert her royal charges.

That unhurried departure from the Palace was to be the last free action of royalty in France for twenty-one years; never again would they have a home of their own, or a garden, and only one of them, Madame Royale, would survive the Revolution which by this act of capitulation they had that day confirmed. It was, in fact, the beginning of the end for Louis XVI and his Queen.

Shortly after they had left the gardens the roar of cannon, the crackle of muskets, and the shouts of a multitude, followed by a slow cloud of smoke drifting over the roofs and domes of the Tuileries, told the frightened Parliamentarians and the Royal Family who had taken refuge among them that the attack on the Palace had begun. The fierce men and women from Marseilles and the hungry mobs from the Faubourg de St. Antoine had broken into the Palace from the Carrousel, the courtyard on the eastern side, and were now engaged in hand-to-hand combat with the thousand Swiss guards and a few hundred National Guards who had remained behind to defend the family. By ten o'clock it was all over; the abandoned Swiss lay massacred and mutilated throughout the Palace, on the steps, and in the pleasant gardens; the mob, mad with excitement and liquor, proceeded to sack the Palace from end to end. Terrible things were done that day which I will not try to describe.

In the Riding School, as the Royal Family entered, the heat was already oppressive; the semi-circular benches were crowded with deputies, and the public galleries were crammed. Vergniaud, orator of the Gironde, was in the chair, and he solemnly assured Louis that he and his family would have the full protection of Parliament from the roaring mob outside. The party were shown in to the little reporters' box behind the President and to his right. It was, says Lenôtre, barely ten feet square, with iron bars in front. In this little place, with hostile deputies taking every opportunity to insult them, with the stench of unwashed people inside and outside the Riding School rising to their nostrils, and under a blazing August sun which turned the old building into a furnace, the Royal Family were forced to remain from shortly before nine in the morning till past midnight. Then, half fainting from hunger, thirst, and anxiety, they were led away for the night to two barely furnished rooms in the nearby monastery of the Feuillants.

The King, as always, managed to sleep; the children were already asleep, the Dauphin being carried from the Riding School; the others slept from time to time, except the Queen. All through the early morning hours Marie-Antoinette lay furious and humiliated on an iron bedstead and would not be consoled. It was full light when at last she fell uneasily to sleep for the few remaining hours before they were taken back to the reporters' box in the Riding School.

That day, Saturday the eleventh, was a repetitive nightmare of the first, only that they were permitted to retire into a little ante-chamber for food and drink, where a few faithful gentlemen of the bodyguard had received permission to watch over them.

They spent the second night, and the third, in the same rooms of the Feuillants; during the fourth day, Monday the thirteenth, the debate to which they were forced to listen was almost all concerned with what was to be done with them—some were for lodging them in the Luxembourg, others for some other Parisian prison; eventually, it was decided that they should all be sent to the Tower of the old Temple fortress, one of the northern bastions of the city, from which it would be difficult to rescue them—if by chance there were any left to dare it.

That evening, about dusk, they were loaded into two great carriages (Lenôtre mentions one carriage only) for the drive to the Temple, some two miles' distant. They crossed the Place Vendôme and on into the main streets of the city, through hostile, bloodthirsty multitudes who crowded to the windows to shout filthy insults, particularly to the Queen, whom they loathed; heads on pikes were thrust before their eyes.

As the slow, tortured journey dragged through two hours the King sat mute and outwardly unmoved—in his honest, puzzled mind the thought was uppermost that he was no longer King of France, for he had heard the Act of Deposition with his own ears in the Assembly. We may be sure too that his mind dwelt with great sadness on the fate of his wife and his two children, and of his sister who was with them in the carriage—of his own fate he was always unconcerned.

So they passed through Paris together for the last time, at each street corner meeting new crowds, more insults, greater humiliations. Inside their carriage they sat, helpless and perspiring, in the odorous summer warmth of the Paris streets. At last the cavalcade rolled into the long, ancient and sinister rue du Temple, and turning to the left made even slower progress until it reached the place from which rose the forbidding buildings and towers of the Temple.

Here their carriage stopped. With much difficulty, and amid uproar from the crowds gathered to gloat over their downfall, they were unloaded into the street and escorted through the big door into the courtyard, up the steps into the main building, out of sight. The doors were shut behind them with the hopeless finality of all prison doors; they were led along a last passage into the open, and so to the great Tower itself, "with lamps in every old crocket of the corners, and every window ablaze." [Hilaire Belloc.]

ii

It was, as I have said, Monday, August 13, 1792, when they entered the Temple Tower which was to be their last home together. Here, under constant and often brutally insensitive surveillance, they remained until Monday, January 20, 1793, when Louis was taken to the guillotine in the Place de la Révolution. Marie-Antoinette was removed on August 2 of that year to the Conciergerie Prison, on the Ile de la Cité, there to await her trial, and at length, on October 16, her death, on the same scaffold and in the same place. Mme. Elisabeth, left alone with the two children, eventually followed the brother and sister-in-law she had loved so well, and for whom she suffered so much, and was buried in the cemetery of the Madeleine where today the Chapelle Expiatoire tells their mournful story.

The Dauphin, to Royalists the lawful Louis XVII of France, died alone in the grim tower, his little frame rotten with the rickets which inhuman gaolers and a frightened government did nothing to arrest. Much has been written to prove that the Dauphin did not die in the Temple, and numerous imposters appeared in later years who claimed to be the son of Marie-Antoinette. Expert opinion, on the whole, disbelieves this story.

Only Madame Royale, his sister, afterwards the Duchesse d'Angoulême, miraculously escaped and lived to hold in her trembling hand, a quarter of a century later her mother's letter, written in the damp Conciergerie cell on the morning of her execution.

iii

Barely a week of the Royal Family's captivity had passed before the Paris Commune, who throughout had official charge of the royal prisoners, ordered the arrest of the Princesse de Lamballe and the Duchesse de Tourzel, thus depriving the King and Queen of the last of their friends, and ensuring that no one of their own rank and intelligence should remain with them.

The family was now alone, with the exception of Hue, a valet (who was soon removed also and replaced by another, Cléry, of whom we shall hear more) and a vile man named Tison and his wife, spies of the Commune, besides the two Municipal officers who watched them night and day, and who were changed frequently.

At first the prisoners were lodged in the Little Tower, which backed on to the Great Tower like a small brother. After September 30, they were transferred to rooms on the second and third floors of the Great Tower which had been hastily prepared for them. Of their life of isolation in this ancient and gloomy building, we have fortunately a complete and detailed account consisting of the "Journal," written in simple and moving language by Cléry, which was translated into English and published in London in 1798, and re-published in 1955 by the Folio Society, London. There is no reason to doubt its authenticity, and since all historians have accepted it as genuine, and quoted it extensively, we may find in it a faithful picture of their daily life, and learn of the heights and depths of which man is capable in times of greatest stress.

Cléry had been a valet in the royal service for ten years and was actually in charge of the Dauphin when the Tuileries was attacked by the mob on August 10. He was not allowed to go with him to the Riding School, and on that day nearly lost his life several times. He contrived to escape, and at length reached his home in

Versailles after much danger and anxiety, and a few days later, on hearing that the Royal Family were alone in the Tower, offered his services to the Mayor of Paris as valet to the King. He was conducted to the Tower on August 26, and at once attended Louis, "dressing him in the morning and rolling his hair at night."

This brave man remained with the Royal Family for five long and terrible months, ministering to their needs as best he could, comforting them with such good news as he was able to learn through the courage of his wife who brought the clean linen every week, tending them when they fell ill, combing their hair, playing games with the Dauphin, to whom he was devoted, and, when Louis was separated from his family on September 29, maintaining contact between him and the Queen until some days later they were permitted to take their meals together once more.

He slept always at Louis' bedside, brought him the news of his forthcoming trial, and on numerous occasions defied the stupid and often vicious officers who ordered him from time to time to do things which would humiliate his master and mistress.

It was Cléry who arranged the chairs in the King's dining room for the last reunion of Louis with his wife, sister and children on the eve of his death, watched over him that night as he slept peacefully till at five in the morning Louis woke to the sound of the crackling of the wood burning in the fire which Cléry had lit; and at the last, at half-past eight, in pale daylight, he embraced the King "and bathed him with tears" as Santerre led him away to the troops outside.

A short walk in the open brought the little party to a large closed carriage, and as soon as the King and the Abbé Edgeworth, with two armed guards, were seated, the trumpets sounded and the procession started. It was led by a large number of drummers. The route of about two miles was lined by troops and armed companies of citizens. Of spectators there were none. All other street movement had been prohibited in the centre of Paris, and most people stayed in their houses. In a silent city and through closed shutters far and wide they heard from time to time the throbbing of the drums, and there were many who shivered at the meaning of it.

We can follow the probable route without difficulty, for the streets are still there:

From the Temple along the little rue Meslay, eastwards across the rue St. Martin, over what is now the junction of the Boulevards Sébastopol and Strasbourg, then in front of the Portes St. Martin and St. Denis to the top of the rue de Cléri (now 'Clery'). Here a desperate loyalist, de Batz, had stationed himself with a few friends. As the procession passed, they broke through the troops and rushed towards the carriage. Three were cut down at once; the others, including de Batz, escaped. The King continued to read his breviary, and gave no sign of having seen the attempt to save him. The late M. Georges Cain, Director of the Carnavalet Museum, describes this incident, as do a number of other authorities, but the Abbé Edgeworth makes no mention of it in his account of the journey to the scaffold.

On they went down the winding narrow street (it is the same today for its northern half) along the short rue du Mail, past the Place des Victoires—where six months later Charlotte Corday alighted from the Caen coach on her mission to assassinate Marat—into the rue des Petits Champs, through the Place Vendôme, and along the rue Royale, with the great *place*, packed tight with a buzzing mass of people, in front of them. As the procession debouched into the wide space of the square the rolling of the drums increased in violence, flooding the air with menace and drowning all other sounds in that vast, expectant place.

In the chilly morning air the Place de la Révolution (Concorde) was as we know it today, but without its obelisk. Where this now rises up there stood a broad pedestal, from which a statue of Louis XV had been hacked down. Half-way between this and the entrance to the Champs Elysées the guillotine was erected for the King. [Other sites have been quoted, but the words in the special Proclamation of the day previous are clear: "*La Place de la Révolution, ci-devant Louis XV, entre le pied-d'estal et les Champs Elysées.*"] The carriage with its escort lumbered over to the west side, and there, in front of Marly's famous pillared horses, with all the

drums still rolling, the King paid with dignity and courage for his grievous faults.

iv

In 1808, by order of the government, the Great Tower of the Temple, with its turret walls nine feet thick, was pulled down. Inside those walls, while they contained the King and his family, destiny had unfolded, heavy with misfortune. They encompassed the lowest meanness, the greatest generosity; dignity, courage and base cowardice; the grinding sorrow and the fragile happiness of a devoted family waiting for death; the laughter and tears of a little boy and the despair of a mother's cries; the hopes and fears of one of Europe's famous reigning families, reduced to the status of criminals from whom every personal article of value and sentiment was taken. Surely no other bricks and mortar, as they crashed to dust under the housebreakers' sledge hammers, had housed a sharper grief, a nobler fortitude!

Today the Square du Temple contains a pleasant public garden, with trees and a lake; in the hot summer afternoons the place is full of children who play hide and seek, dangle their legs on swings and seesaws, and draw pictures with their toes in the numerous sandpits put there for their enjoyment by an enlightened municipality. Their mothers sit under the shade of the trees and watch them (as Marie-Antoinette had fearfully watched hers in the same place), knit as mothers always knit, and gossip with each other. Truck drivers blast the peace of the place with the sound of their clamant horns; from the big Mairie, on the eastern side of the square, squat young Parisian policemen go on their business of keeping law and order in the district. Sometimes when the weather is good a band plays in the gardens.

The tiny rue du Fôrez, on the north-east corner, and the big house on the rue Charlot looking down it straight to the site of the Tower on the corner of the rue Perrée and the rue Eugène Spuller, are in almost every detail exactly as they were when the carriage brought the royal prisoners to the Temple; behind every shuttered window of these old houses people shivered in the early morning cold of January 21, 1793 to listen to the troops form up and the carriage roll over the gravel to take the King away.

Today you can stand on the pavement and look up to the open sky where the Tower stood, and project yourself back into the King's dining room on the second floor the night before he died, where for nearly two anguished hours he sat with his family, and embraced them for the last time; where he took the little Dauphin in his arms and made him swear never to try to avenge his father's death; and into the shattered Queen's bedroom, directly over his, in which she waited in vain to hold him in her arms once more on that last morning of his life; and into which, an hour or so later, came up to her the shrill voice of the news-vendor crying: "*Le Tyran est mort! Vive la Nation! Vive la République!*"

You can ponder on all these things among the ancient houses and streets which were there when they happened; you can walk slowly down the dark and narrow rue du Temple, and hear the knife-grinder's bell as

Louis heard it in his carriage, his hands crossed, his confession made, his mind serene, as he left the Tower to face the end.

As I walked slowly down the street a newsboy began calling from a corner of the Square: "*Paris Soir! Paris Soir! Le Gouvernement et la Crise!*" And I thought, which Government? Which Crisis?

Echoes, echoes, always these strange echoes!

Fouquier de Tinville, Public Prosecutor of the Terror

11. DUNGEON OF THE QUEEN

The Conciergerie Prison

i

Between April 1793 and July 1794, 3,958 men and women were beheaded in Paris. Of these, 1,351 died in the last month of the Terror under Robespierre's ruthless Law of Prairial, which deprived the accused of witnesses, and indeed of any trial at all beyond a brief appearance before the Revolutionary Tribunal to answer their names, be insulted, and sentenced to die the same day. At the height of the Terror, Fouquier-Tinville, the public prosecutor, said that he must have thirty, forty, fifty and even sixty accused every day. And he had them.

We must turn to our own enlightened century to find such planned ferocity.

Why did it have to happen? What was this Revolutionary Tribunal, and where did it sit? And who was this man, this tiger Fouquier-Tinville, whose name is tied to its excesses forever?

The Tribunal was set up in March, 1793 by the National Convention out of fear—fear of reprisals for the carnage of the September massacres of the previous year. The surging passions let loose by the Revolution swept its leaders on from one desperate act to another. Everything was at stake—the revolution itself, the nation now at war with the greatest powers in Europe; the lives of the ruthless and largely inexperienced men at the head of affairs hung by a thread. The Duke of Brunswick, in command of the invading armies, had issued a decree which left none of them in any doubt of their fate if they lost the war; and, most potent, most pressing factor of all, Paris was short of food and would soon get out of hand.

In this atmosphere it was all or nothing, and the strongest revolutionary leaders had no difficulty in deciding that two policies were essential. At the front there must be ceaseless energy and a fierce determination to win the war; at home they must strike terror into the hearts of all who were not actively of the same mind as themselves—the classic prescriptions for a revolution at the cross-roads.

And time was short, as well as food. The enemy, already far into French soil, must be thrown back now—this very week, this very month, while in Paris no risk whatever must be taken with anyone who might try to stage a counter-revolution. Better that some of the innocent should die with the guilty, if that were the price of victory.

Thus was this Tribunal of the Terror set to work, with new laws, new judges, new jurymen, and an unknown prosecutor who had ambitions and a large family to feed, and whose appointment was fortuitous because the senior prosecutor of Paris pleaded ill-health and inability for such a task. Danton urged the Tribunal on; "Let us profit by the errors of our predecessors. Let us be terrible, to spare the people being terrible!"

A year later, on trial before this same Tribunal, he was to ask the pardon of God and man for his part in its inception, and in April, 1795, exactly one year later still, Fouquier-Tinville and Herman, Danton's judge, were shaking with rage as a reformed Tribunal stripped them of all their offices and sent them to the guillotine to follow the thousands they had condemned. The mills of God ground quickly enough in the ancient Palace of the Kings on the Ile de la Cité.

The victims of the Tribunal came from every quarter and every class. Some, like the deputies of the Gironde, were spewed from power because they refused to accept that liberty could only be won by brutality; others were aristocrats or known Royalists; many more were innocent wretches plucked from home and family because of hearsay, or some act of spite by someone with whom they had quarrelled. The police spies of the Committee of Public Safety were everywhere, and they had orders to provide the Tribunal with work.

When a man or woman was arrested it was generally at home. Brutally seized, given only a few moments—not always that—to say farewell to husband, wife, and children, the prisoner was bundled into a carriage and taken to the Conciergerie Prison, a fearful, stinking clutter of cells and dark chambers situated directly under the rooms where the Revolutionary Tribunal sat, on the first floor of the Palace of Justice.

Here the victim was received, registered, and flung into a dungeon with hundreds of others like him, to await the day when the Public Prosecutor and his assistants pricked his name on tomorrow's lists to go before the Tribunal. So swiftly did Fouquier work that it was seldom that any one in this hell on earth had long to wait. There was, as some of them said, something to thank God for in that.

A few—they can be numbered on two hands—heard, to their amazement, the clerks ordered to strike their names from the indictment—"You are Innocent, Citizen," and in a daze they found themselves outside, engulfed in the cheers and embraces of the mobs who hung like leeches on the great stairways of the Palace.

But to most the summons in the evening, when the Court Officials went round calling out the names for tomorrow's trials, meant a last night on earth and only part of a last day to follow. All these, without exception, began their journey to the scaffold from this building and here they awaited the clanging of the bell in the little courtyard which announced the arrival outside of the carts to take them to the place of execution.

For this was the beginning of the Way of the Tumbrils, which we shall follow later. Before we take our place, let us examine this rat-ridden, tear-laden prison more closely, with its three grim towers—Bonbec, César, d'Argent; its great room in which the judges spun a man to his death in the space of a few minutes, often with a jest or a gibe to add good measure; its creaking wicket-gates and damp dark dungeons; its winding stairways and echoing corridors; its old doorway leading to nine broad stone steps where at the top the death carts waited for their appointed batches, with Sanson, the executioner, list in hand; above him the howling fiends with filth in their mouths and in their hands, who day after day fed their appetite for cruelty by mocking the men and women on their way to the scaffold.

These, dragging their feet into the daylight, their hands bound behind their backs, went up the steps and into the tumbrils in every state of mind from the serene to the terrible. But for the most part, knowing how near they were to the end, they bore themselves with dignity, and on their suffering faces was a look of the beyond.

ii

The Palace of Justice at the time of the Revolution consisted of three floors. At ground level was the prison and above were the various Courts, with judge's and lawyer's rooms on either side. The prison included two open spaces—the men's courtyard and the women's courtyard, the first running nearly the whole length of the building from north to south, and the second, much smaller and at the back, from east to west. On either side of the men's courtyard were numerous cells, and a long narrow place for those unable to pay for a cell flanked it on its eastern side.

Behind the entrance to the Conciergerie was a maze of smaller rooms, divided from each other by dirty glass partitions or by iron grilles, according to their use. A long dingy corridor ran east to west to connect these places with the women's courtyard on the left side, and the cells and the men's courtyard on the right. Running parallel with the latter was a glass-covered walk way, where the prisoners awaiting trial could spend a few daylight hours in exercise and conversation.

For those who inhabited the dreary cells for the last few days of their lives, life was just possible. They could at least undress and sleep in twos and threes, and there was some elementary privacy. But for the mass of human beings who were thrown into the main dungeon, life was bearable only because release by death was at hand. They were crammed together in thirties and forties where only a quarter that number could lie down at one time. Those who could, spent the night standing up, but hundreds, exhausted by their experiences, fell on top of those already lying down. There was practically no ventilation, sanitary arrangements were completely inadequate, and the wretched straw mattresses were rarely changed, so that for most of the time they were verminous, and worse. From all this concourse of human misery an indescribable stench arose and remained by day and night.

The women were better off, though nothing of comfort or real privacy from each other was possible. They were able to make some kind of toilet, and to wash their clothes from a tap in their courtyard (it is still there). During the day, if the weather was fine, they could walk about and at certain times converse with the other prisoners from behind the iron railings which separated the women's courtyard from a small open space near the main corridor.

There exist many descriptions of the life these abandoned people led. Some were light-headed; others recited poetry, talked philosophy, the arts, and even of the political turmoil outside which was responsible for them being where they were. Many walked, sat, or lay in silence, their minds a blank or lost in the past. Some could not restrain their grief and terror, and their cries reached every part of the prison.

There was always plenty of movement in the place. New prisoners were arriving at all times of the day and night, and the noisy process of handing them through the various wicket-gates and pushing them into the cells or dungeons went on continuously. Every evening the prisoners gathered in expectant groups to listen to the officials from the Revolutionary Tribunal calling out the names for the next day's trials. As this man and that woman heard their names, they gave way to loud cries, fell to the stone floor, embraced those nearest to them, or laughed, or stood in silence, or fell on their knees and prayed.

Fouquier-Tinville and his assistants worked late and at great pressure to prepare the lists for each day's trials. The Public Prosecutor had his office in the Tour Bonbec, on the second floor, and lived in a set of rooms in the Tour d'Argent, both towers facing the river on the northern side of the Palace.

This man, in the middle forties, was a competent, hard-working lawyer who by chance found himself in the very centre of the judicial machine which the government had erected, with the injunction that it should be swift and terrible. He believed it to be his duty to see that the lists were filled each night, and he succeeded in stifling his doubts, if he had any, about the impartiality of the justice he served out with such unfailing regularity.

He sat till the early hours of the morning in his office writing out the names on the sheets of paper, framing the indictments (they were all much alike, but he insisted that they should be done) checking and re-checking that these names were represented by the helpless flesh and blood below. I say "represented," because there were tragic cases where the wrong people had been arrested, sons for fathers, daughters for mothers. Fouquier was not too particular about such things. "If this man is here," he would say sharply on some error being hinted at, "we shall soon find if he is guilty or not."

When his time came to stand his own trial it was these inhumanities that trapped him. Husbands and wives, brothers and sisters, bereaved without the slightest reason except that Fouquier had put their loved ones on his list, crowded in to witness against him, shouting their curses. "Assassin! Fiend! Give me back my father! Where is my beloved wife?" These were the cries that drained the blood from his sallow face and stopped his legal pleading that he had only acted under the orders of the Committee of Public Safety, that his own head would have gone if he had done otherwise, which was true.

When the tumbril took him to the scaffold in front of the Town Hall on the other side of the river Paris went wild with joy. Only his last letter to his wife and children remains to prove that human blood and not iced water ran in his tight veins:

"I send you in my portfolio a letter containing my feelings towards you, and two others which you will deliver, in time, if there is an opportunity. Do not grieve, they are the feelings engraven on my heart that I send you, and that, perhaps, I may not have another opportunity of conveying to you. Shall I, perhaps, be happier? Shall I display them in person? I hope so; but at such a juncture we must expect anything. That is why I have arrived at this decision. Once more, do not be troubled.

"I kiss you with all my heart. Keep well. I kiss aunt and the children."

His was a small, pedantic mind, streaked with cruelty,

and it is to be doubted if he realized the part he was playing in history. He regarded himself as the servant of others infinitely more powerful. That is the most that can be said in his favor, if anything need be.

iii

On August 2, 1793 in the early hours, officers of the Committee of Public Safety came to the Temple to tell the Queen that she was to stand her trial for treason, and ordered her without delay to go with them. A hurried embrace with her children, an agonising farewell to Madame Elisabeth her sister-in-law, now to be left alone with her son and daughter, and she was taken down those winding stairs from which she had heard the last faint steps of the King eight months earlier.

A carriage took her swiftly down the darkened rue du Temple, rattled across the wide Place de Crève and over the Pont au Change to the huge shape of the prison on the island. The gates of the Cour du Mai opened and shut, she was hurried down the steps, passed the rough clerk's office, signed for ("the widow Capet; age, 38"), and lodged in a small cell looking, through a heavily-barred window almost on ground level, onto the stone floor of the women's courtyard. In the light of two candles she could see only the barest furnishings, and lay down on the iron bed they had provided for the former Queen of France.

Throughout a hot August she remained in this small place. Little daylight came through the window, but she could see the feet and legs of other women as they walked in the courtyard outside. Each day she rose and dressed with care, for she had been permitted a fairly ample wardrobe. Each night she undressed herself, hung her clothes across the back of the chair and lay down to try to sleep.

Apart from her surroundings, she was well cared for. The gaoler's wife was kind and did what she could for her, and in the matter of food and drink the Queen had whatever she wished, the dishes being cooked specially. Even so, she ate and drank little, spoke seldom, and cried every time the woman brought her own little son in to see the Queen. What hurt her most was the presence, every moment of the day and night, of a police officer and a guard, who lived, ate their meals, and slept always in sight of her.

After the first week they took away her few personal belongings, except a lock of the Dauphin's hair which she hid in the bosom of her dress. She suffered much from an excess of bleeding, and they sent Souberbielle the surgeon to her—he who was on the jury at Danton's trial, and was to sit a few weeks later as a juryman to hear the case against her also. He made a report to the people who sent him, but she was given no treatment, nor asked for any.

Her eyesight began to fail, in one eye particularly; her auburn hair, always the most carefully tended part of her toilet at Versailles, turned rapidly grey; she looked thirty years beyond her age.

At the end of August she was taken from this cell and relodged in another on the other side of the courtyard. Her guards went with her, passing their time and hers playing *piquet*, and walking up and down the cell or along the passage outside. Only a small screen separated them from their prisoner. For most of the day the Queen sat on her bed or the one chair, as though already in another world. Sometimes she read a little of the books they brought her.

A girl, Rosalie Lamorlière, served her meals and tended to her daily needs. This child later testified in some detail concerning the last few weeks of Marie Antoinette's short life. There is a tenderness in her tale that shows how the dignity and, at the last, the nobility of this Princess of Austria captured the heart of the only servant now left to her.

Through September and into October the days passed with the same monotony and sense of finality. The Queen had long since lost hope of seeing her children again, or indeed of anything at all except the end she knew was being prepared for her.

There was, for a brief and astonishing twenty-four hours, a plan to rescue her. A man was smuggled into her cell who left her a message in some flowers. One of the guards was in the plot, but either from fear or for reward gave the game away; the days went by and the Queen heard no more.

On October 12 the last stage of her pilgrimage began when she was taken up to the floor above for a preliminary examination. She answered all the questions put to her mechanically, and returned to her cell to await her trial, now fixed to begin in two days' time. Two counsel were assigned to her defence, and unwillingly she spent some hours with them, listening dully to them while they explained the nature of the charges she must face, and consenting to go through the legal papers they were preparing for her. On October 14 she was taken up into the long room where the Revolutionary Tribunal sat waiting; the President was Herman, the prosecutor Fouquier-Tinville himself.

Fouquier, as always, had left nothing to chance. Though her earlier record of extravagance and lack of judgment, and her later correspondence with the enemy were all known and could not be contradicted, the Prosecutor of the Terror had prepared his case with special care. The list of witnesses included servants from Versailles, shopkeepers, hairdressers, soldiers, and politicians. The law must always be rigorously applied, but in this case the evidence must be exact.

The Committee had ordered her trial for another reason than plain hatred. By bringing her before the Revolutionary Tribunal they had challenged the invading powers, hoping that these would halt their armies as the price for Marie Antoinette's freedom. It was in vain, for no such bargain was ever hinted at. The Austrians realised that she was doomed, and pressed their armies on, the total destruction of the young Republic being now their goal. The fiends in Paris had already murdered the King, and the time for bargaining was over. The half-blind Hapsburg woman in the Conciergerie must therefore stand her trial, and her execution would add another crime for which the Prussians and the Austrians would exact a fearful vengeance.

The trial of Marie Antoinette, like all the other great events of the Revolution, has been described in every detail by many historians and in almost every language. The rasp of Herman's voice, the dreary procession of witnesses trailing through the Court to tell of this remark and that by "the Austrian woman," the ghastly indecencies with which the fanatical Hébert sought to debauch the Queen, and her despairing cry: "I appeal to every mother here," the over-careful questioning by Fouquier, and the Queen's exhausted but dignified bearing through hour after hour of purgatory—these may all be read at length elsewhere.

At four o'cock on the morning of October 16, the Queen was found guilty on all the indictments and sentenced to death, the execution to take place at midday. She was led back to her cell, and there, drawing strength from some inner spring yet untapped, she sat down to write that last letter to the King's sister which, in its simple words and noble thought, atoned for everything that had gone before and has put her among the immortals. Today it is in the National Archives (60 rue des Francs-Bourgeois) where they will show you a facsimile. The original is kept locked in a lead case.

October 16th, at half past four in the morning.

It is to you, Sister, that I am writing for the last time. I have just been sentenced to death, but not to a shameful one, since this death is shameful only to criminals, whereas I am going to rejoin your brother. Innocent like him, I hope to show the firmness which he showed during his last moments. I am calm, as one may well be when one's conscience is clear, though deeply grieved at having to forsake my poor children. You know that I existed only for them and for you, my good and affectionate sister. You who, in the kindness of your heart, had sacrificed everything in order to be with us—in what a terrible position do I leave you! It was only during the trial that I learned my daughter had been separated from you. Alas, poor child, I do not dare write to her, for she would not receive my letter; I do not even know if this one will reach you. However, through you I send them both my blessing, in the hope that some day, when they are older, they will be with you once more and will be able to enjoy your tender care. If only they will both continue to think the thoughts with which I have never ceased to inspire them, namely that sound principles and the exact performance of duties are the prime foundation of life, and that mutual love and confidence will bring them happiness. I trust my daughter will feel that at the age she has now reached she must always help her brother with the advice which her greater experience and her affection will enable her to give him; and that my son, in his turn, will give his sister all the care and will do her all the services which affection can stimulate; that they will both of them feel, whatever position they may find themselves in, they cannot be truly happy unless united—that they will take example from us. In our misfortunes, how much consolation we have derived from our mutual affection! Again, in happy times, one's enjoyment is doubled when one can share it with a friend—and where can one find a more affectionate, a more intimate friend than in one's own family? I hope my son will never forget his father's last words which I here purposely repeat for him: Let him never try to avenge our death!

I have to speak to you of one matter which is extremely painful. I know how much my little boy must have made you suffer. Forgive him, my dear sister; remember how young he is, and how easy it is to make a child say whatever one wants, to put words he does not understand into his mouth. I hope a day will come when he will grasp the full value of your kindnesses and of the affection you have shown both my children.

It remains to entrust you with my last thoughts. I should have liked to write them before the trial opened; but, apart from the fact that I was not allowed to write, things have moved so swiftly that I really have not had time.

I die in the Catholic, Apostolic, and Roman religion, in that of my fathers, that in which I was brought up, and which I have always professed. Having no hope of any spiritual consolation, not even knowing whether there are still priests of this religion in France, and feeling that should there be such I should expose them to great risks were they to visit me here, I sincerely ask God's forgiveness for all the faults I have committed since I was born. I trust that, in His goodness, He will hear my last prayers, as well as those which I have long been making that, in His pity and His goodness, He may receive my soul.

I ask the forgiveness of all those whom I have known, and, especially of you, my sister, for the sorrow which, unwittingly, I may have caused them. I forgive my enemies the evil they have done me. I here bid farewell to my aunts and to my brothers and sisters. I had friends. The thought of being separated from them for ever and of their distresses is among my greatest regrets in dying. Let them know, at least, that down to the last they were in my mind.

Adieu, my good and affectionate sister. I trust that this letter will reach you. Continue to think of me. I send you my most heartfelt love, and also to my poor, dear children. How heartbreaking it is to leave them for ever! Adieu, adieu, I must now devote myself entirely to my spiritual duties. Since all my actions are under restraint, it is possible that they will bring a priest to me. I declare, however, that I shall not say a word to him, and that I shall treat him as an absolute stranger.*

* From *Marie-Antoinette* by Stefan Zweig, translated by Eden and Cedar Paul, The Viking Press, Inc., New York: 1933.

When she had finished, she lay down and wept as she had shed no tears before. The girl Rosalie stood by her bedside, begging her to taste a little vermicelli soup she had made specially for her. The Queen raised herself to take a spoonful, and, still crying, put her head once more on the pillow. Later she slept a little, until the time came for her to make ready. Then she changed into a clean white dress, put some rouge on her sunken cheeks, and suffered her hair to be cut short without protest. Only when they went to bind her hands she asked them why. "They did not bind the King's hands," she pleaded. The gaoler's wife wrapped a scarf round her shoulders, and on her head the Queen put a plain white cap. Rather like a child going resignedly to some new school, she walked out of the cell in which we shall shortly stand, went up the steps which led to Sanson and the waiting tumbril, and passed out into streets lined by thirty thousand soldiers and filled with the roaring people.

As she passed down the rue St. Honoré, Jacques-Louis David, the artist of the Revolution, rapidly sketched her from a window above. This little drawing, now in the Louvre Museum, has been the subject of controversy. David was an ardent revolutionary and a member of the Jacobins club. In a few lines he gives the Queen's figure all the poverty and misery of which his genius was capable. Her face sags in a mixture of anger and contempt; beneath the white cap perched clumsily on top of her head a few straggling hairs protrude. When, in 1948, this sketch was included in the centenary exhibition of David's paintings at the Tate Gallery, the *Times* in an

Conciergerie Prison

12. THE MOUSETRAP

Hell on Earth

i

I recommend the visitor to the Conciergerie to station himself first of all on the north bank of the river, half way between the Pont Neuf to the west and the Pont au Change to the east. From the Louvre, via the Quai du Louvre and the Quai de la Mégisserie is a short and pleasant walk, and it is on the last-named embankment that I would have you stand for a few minutes.

Opposite, across the Seine, the great mass of the Palace

of Justice straddles the space between the two bridges, and the three conical towers mark the site and extent on the Quai de l'Horloge of the old Conciergerie prison. Immediately to the left of the Tour de César is a small tunnel-like gateway. This is the modern entrance to the prison, and we shall pass through here in a little while. The entrance and exit at the time of the Revolution, which I have described, were at the eastern side of the Palace, past the southern end of the Pont au Change, the bridge now on your left.

Had we been standing here at the end of the eighteenth century the buildings opposite would have looked rather different. The three towers were there, and the slender steeple of the Ste. Chapelle in the left background; but in front of the present uniform three stories of stone was a hotch-potch of old structures of all shapes and sizes, partly hiding the prison and taking up most of the present roadway of the Quai de l'Horloge.

As with so much of Revolutionary Paris, the housebreakers were busily at work during the last century, and all this fascinating rabbit-warren of old buildings which had seen and heard so much was swept away to make the river frontage respectable. It was then that the real gateway of the prison on the Boulevard du Palais was walled up and the present small entrance by the Tour de César pierced through. We and posterity are the losers, because so much of what we see today is modern and we can be sadly misled unless we know how to look, and where.

All the same, standing where we are and sweeping the whole scene in front of us with a knowledgeable eye, we can feel strongly the heavy, brooding atmosphere of this place; we can imagine Fouquier-Tinville at work on his lists late at night over there in the Tour de Bonbec, project ourselves past the twin towers into the hall where the Revolutionary Tribunal sat eating up the lives of fifty people a day, and think for a moment that on the floor beneath, behind the modern facade of windows facing us, lay the dungeon, crammed with wretched people who had only a few days to live.

Here, almost in the shadow of Notre Dame, with the great petrol barges plying peacefully past its walls amid the sight and sound of omnibuses and all the paraphernalia of modern life, we are looking at the headquarters of the Terror.

ii

Let us now retrace our steps westwards along the Quai de la Mégisserie and cross the Pont Neuf. On the south bank the brick house facing us at the end of the Quai de l'Horloge was the birthplace and early home of Mme. Roland. A plaque giving the details is fixed beneath one of the upper windows—one of the few of its kind I have seen in Paris. (How much kinder to the seeker after such things is London.)

We should turn left here, and walk past the old shops which face the river for the first hundred yards or so. There are a printer, several book shops, a window filled with antiques, and one which announces, in old white letters turned yellow with age, that *Execution Rapide* is offered here. It is not what we think—merely an optician who has found words in tune with his *locale* to say how quickly he can make your spectacles. Well, we are past the three towers, and here, on the right, is the new entrance to the Conciergerie which we could see from the north bank.

We pass through the gloomy archway and find ourselves in a small courtyard surrounded by the high buildings on all sides. In this space stood the prison kitchens. On the right is a doorway through which the visitor today gains his entrance to the prison itself.

Stand for a moment and look up at the first floor windows above. There is a glimpse of a decorated ceiling, and you can see that light is also coming from windows on the other side. You are looking at the site of the courtroom of the Revolutionary Tribunal—much altered, but it was there. Now turn and let your eye wander over the back of the tower—here we are close to the Public Prosecutor's offices.

We ring the bell, the door opens, and stepping over a low wooden partition, we pass through a kind of wire-netted office in which there is a turnstile, with the invariable ageing woman, a shawl round her shoulders, who takes your francs and gives you a scruffy paper ticket in exchange.

The brightness of the day outside emphasises the darkness within, and it is only after a moment or two of peering about that we perceive we are in an enormous underground enclosure stretching away in all directions. We are in fact in the onetime kitchens and great hall of the ancient royal palace. Enormous Gothic pillars support the whole building, their classic shapes dissolving into darkness as they reach the ceilings for above us. On the opposite side is the narrow entrance to a winding stairway leading to the courtrooms above—to the hall of the Tribunal itself. This is (wrongly) called the Stairway of the Queen, and the voluble old guide, when he has dismissed the party he now leads back towards the turnstile, will tell us that it was by these stairs that Marie Antoinette went up to face her implacable judges and Fouquier-Tinville with his lists and his saturnine countenance. Normally we should stand around and wait—a little nervously perhaps—for the guide, refreshed by his tips, to approach us in our turn. Today we may dispense with his services, if you will allow me to take his place.

iii

When the departing group of visitors is ejected, the woman at the turnstile closes the outer wooden door, slams the turnstile, and with a horrible grating noise

—LOCKS IT. We look at each other. Is this all right? There are such things as ghosts we think for a cowardly second. This is a strange place, full of dark shadows and guttering echoes. We shiver a little.

And well we may, for where we now stand was the terrible *Souricière*—the Mousetrap. On these cold stone slabs where we walk softly, afraid that the noise of our footsteps may wake some frightened spirit, the moaning bodies of hundreds of men and women lay on the foetid mattresses, criss-cross and on their elbows and on their knees and half-standing, half-falling, and others standing and then falling. As we walk down the long vault, we seem to see the great columns waver, shrink and disappear, to be replaced on both sides by dozens of wooden partitions with creaking doors. In the centre where we pick our way the prisoners huddled in ragged heaps, so that the turnkeys and gaolers going about their business were continually treading on them as they passed up and down. Curses, shrieks and mumbled prayers burdened the sweltering air.

At the far end we can see light coming through a doorway, and gaining this we are now in a long gallery which runs on either side of us. This was the central passage I have spoken of in the last chapter, leading from the old entrance on our left (today a wall separates us from it) through the various wicket-gates; thence on our right it continues to what was called the infirmary, a hellish place where the sick were but little better off than those in the Mousetrap. Along this dim corridor every prisoner came in and went out, hence its name on the old plans as the Prisoners' Gallery.

I know of no place in Paris where the atmosphere is so stiff with dread, the air so still and oppressive, the dirty light so frightening to the eye. In nearly every other place in Revolutionary Paris there are diversions for the eye and mind—the streets full of cars, the pavements with their crowds, the shops and modern buildings, and in these it is a struggle for the imagination to recreate the past. Here, in this dreadful twilight that was of all places in the Revolution the core of misery, the visitor has to fight to keep his sense of being alive. Dampness spreads through the pores of the skin, the sound of our breathing is much too loud, we touch each other suddenly, and recoil.

A few yards to the left is a long black recess. A single dim light hangs from an unseen ceiling. It is about four feet deep and perhaps five or six yards long, and a low wooden bench runs along its length. In front, iron bars form a kind of cage, with a gap in the centre for entrance and exit. It was here that the condemned women had their hair cut off and were made ready for the executioner. On this bench sat Madame Elisabeth the King's sister, Charlotte Corday, Lucille Desmoulins. Bitter tears were shed here, and it is not a place for lingering.

In front of the doorway from the Mousetrap where we emerged into the Prisoners' Gallery, and a little to the right, a stout wooden door faces us. It is reinforced with iron bars, and its great bolts squeak when drawn. Inside is the last dungeon of the Queen. To cross the threshold of this historic place is to experience the feeling that time is really timeless.

We are in a small square room with a low ceiling. In front of us a window looks out onto the women's courtyard, today blocked up with hideous coloured glass. An altar fills the left hand corner of the room, and to the right is the space where the Queen's bed stood; while on a pedestal is displayed a reproduction of the last letter written here by Marie-Antoinette very early on the morning of her death. A doorway on the far side leads to a larger room in which the doomed deputies of the Gironde held their last meeting. Today it is a chapel to their memory. About the middle of the Queen's cell the screen was placed which separated her from the presence of the two men who watched her day and night.

The cell as we see it today has been altered a great deal in everything except its shape. The door originally faced the Queen's bed—i. e., it was on our left as we came in through that entrance which did not exist at the time of the Queen's imprisonment. The altar was placed here long afterwards to mark the place where the Queen's last Mass is believed to have been heard. There was another window, over the bed and facing the Prisoners' Gallery, which has since been blocked up. Of the cell itself as being the place where Marie-Antoinette spent the last weeks and days of her life there is no doubt. Even Lenôtre, who writes so scathingly of the changes in the Conciergerie in *Paris Révolutionnaire*, accepts its authenticity.

It is impossible to put into words the overpowering emotion which you feel as you stand between these four walls. Here, to the right, Rosalie Lamorlière pressed her cup of soup to the Queen's lips; over these few feet of stone floor her poor shrunken body found a few hours of troubled sleep on that last cold morning; through the doorway there they came to take her away. Each of us stands in silence; tragedy crowds the air.

To gain access to the women's courtyard we must pass through the Chapel of the Girondins, and take the small doorway on the left-hand side. Here we step out

Courtyard inside the Conciergerie Prison through which every condemned prisoner passed on the way to the guillotine. Note the bell on the wall to announce the arrival of the tumbrils

into the women's courtyard. The window of the Queen's first cell is the last on the right.

It is worthwhile to give the old iron gateway in front of us more than a glance, for through it passed every woman who died on the scaffold in Paris during the Revolution. It was here that Mme du Barry, crazed with terror, clung desperately to these bars, and it was the jangling of the tumbrils' bell, still hanging high up on the wall opposite, that drowned her wild cries.

Every stone of this menacing place was paced by the feet of those on their way to the guillotine, every bar of that black railing has vibrated to the struggles with which they fought to stave off their last moments, and every foot of these unmerciful walls looked blankly down on them as they look down on us, a century and a half later. Through the right-hand archway they went, the young and the old, the men and the women, and the sound of their wailing voices was carried across to the men's courtyard, and into the crowded, rat-infested Mousetrap, before the heavy walls of the outer prison swallowed them up on their way to the waiting carts on the other side.

We retrace our steps quickly through the Mousetrap to the other end of the long vaulted chamber. If we are lucky we may be able to persuade the old guide to take us up the so-called Stairway of the Queen and unlock the door at the top leading into what is now an ordinary courtroom. Here, as I have said, sat the Revolutionary Tribunal. Nothing at all remains of the chamber of terror as it was, but since we are on the site we will try to re-create the scene.

To our left sit the judges in their black-plumed hats, and in front of them, on a lower level, the Public Prosecutor and his assistants face the crowded public space across the floor at the other end of the room. To the right, in front of where we stand at the top of the stairway, are the four benches on which the prisoners sit.

The jurymen are opposite, and in between are two smaller tables facing each other, one for the defending counsel and the other for the witnesses.

It was in this place that Danton defied Herman, and through these open windows on a quiet spring day his great voice was said to be heard across the river; it was here that in the small hours of the morning Marie-Antoinette heard her sentence; here that so many hundreds of men and women faced the insatiable Fouquier-Tinville and his neat documents of death.

"You do not deny the charge against you, citizen?"

"I do not understand. I have done nothing. I . . ."

"You will understand soon enough, villain. Is it not enough, members of the jury, that this wretch confesses to doing nothing while the fate of France is at stake? You will find him guilty. He is wasting your time."

Almost before the verdict is given the guards hustle him away; the Public Prosecutor bends to his list, spits out a name, and fixes his piercing eyes on another hopeless figure on the benches.

"You are a royalist spy. I have it here in the deposition. We do not need to hear your shameful confession, citizen. . . ."

Only a minute, and he too has gone.

So it goes on, hour after hour, day after day. Fresh spectators crowd in to take the places of those who have heard and seen enough, messengers and officials pass rapidly to and fro, witnesses are pushed forward, speak their false evidence if Fouquier thinks the judges would like to hear it, and disappear. More prisoners come stumbling and shambling on to the benches. From time to time a woman's voice is raised in a shriek as she sees her husband, son, or daughter among the accused.

"Who are you, citizeness? By your cries you betray a guilty conscience."

She is seized, her name taken, and in a moment she is in the toils; in half an hour she is struggling in the Mousetrap below. . . .

We descend the stairs, give the guide his tip, and jostle the turnstile. Will the woman never undo it? Must we remain another minute in this place of horror? Mumbling our farewells we walk quickly out of the now open door, hurry across the little courtyard; and in a moment we see the street outside and a young woman pushing a pram in the sunshine of the living world.

iv

There exists today only one other part of the Conciergerie Prison, the place where the real entrance was, with its little court and short flight of nine steps by which the condemned reached the waiting tumbrils. The same graceful iron railings and tall gates enclose this grim and historic place as they did during the Revolution.

To find it is easy. As we step out of the modern entrance onto the Quai de l'Horloge we must turn right and continue along the Quai for a few yards until we reach the busy Boulevard du Palais, where it joins the southern end of the Pont au Change. Turn right again here, that is, away from the river, and walk along the pavement on the right-hand side of the Boulevard, passing at the corner under the ancient gold and painted clock from which the Quai derives its name. In about a minute we reach the black and gold railings and gates in front of the Palace of Justice, enclosing a courtyard known as the Cour du Mai. No. 18 in the series of prints, *Paris dans sa splendeur*, by Benoist, gives a fine view of this facade. Let us stand outside the centre gates and take a careful look at the railings, the courtyard, the wide steps leading up from it to the four-columned entrance to the Law Courts, and the smaller railings to the right of the main steps.

First, look at the railings and gates directly in front of us. On top of the main gates there is a large golden crest, the principal features of which is the fleur-de-lys. In the centre of the gates the Bourbon emblem is repeated, with a golden crown. The gates on either side are unadorned. Now let us go through those on the right-hand side if they are open (for it was this way that the tumbrils came and went), cross the wide Cour du Mai, and walk to the top of the main steps. From here we can look straight down on the much smaller yard behind the little railings on the right hand side. Where we are standing, the mob stood every day looking down on the tragic procession of people going into the prison on their way to the Revolutionary Tribunal or coming out to begin their last journey. You can see how easy it was to jeer at them and to pelt them with rubbish, and worse.

Today two workmen are unloading casks of wine from a lorry standing where the horse carts once unloaded human beings. Methodically they roll the casks down the steps which Danton and Marie-Antoinette trod, surrounded by soldiers, amid the shouts and curses of the sans-culottes leaning over the balcony above them.

Standing here it is not difficult, with some knowledge of contemporary accounts and prints, to reconstruct the scene, particularly if someone of note is to die. The steps are packed with people, the lucky ones sitting on the balustrade with their legs hanging down on the other side. At the foot of the stairway and right across the main courtyard to the railings are hundreds more, jostling each other to get a better view of the batches in the tumbrils. An officer with plumes in his hat sits on a horse giving directions to the drivers where to place their carts; two are already filled, and the livid-faced men and women sit motionless on the wooden planks. Over on the other side, their backs against the flanking wall of the main building, are more spectators, mostly police, officials of the Committee of Public Safety, and privileged people come to see the spectacle; protruding over the heads of the people here, there, and everywhere are the long thin bayonets of the Republican soldiers.

One cart still waits, backed close up to the railings below us. There is a stirring among the guards in the yard below, a shouted command stills the buzz of the mob, the doors of the prison are flung open, and preceded by a file of soldiers the victims emerge for whom the crowds have massed so tightly. Immediately they come into view the air is bruised with noise and missiles. A young woman dances precariously and suggestively on the balustrade, an old man at the bottom of the steps goes into hysterical paroxysms of laughter. For a moment the central figure in the group of prisoners falters at the sight and sound of the people's fury; a vigorous jab in the back from a soldier jerks him almost on his face; he misses one of the steps, recovers, and at the top he is seized by strong arms and pitched into the tumbril with the others.

When all are loaded the officer on the horse waves his sword and shouts. Sanson himself gets up into one of the carts, and with a crack from his whip each driver sets his load in motion. The three carts move off with difficulty as the mob rushes down from the steps to join the rest of the spectators in the courtyard, and all push and sway as they hem in the little cavalcade to get a closer view and to shout some final obscenity. As the first cart reaches the left-hand gateway it has to stop for a moment as the crowds in the street start to howl and seem likely to break through the soldiers ranked on either side of the street; they are held back and the procession starts again, turning now towards the river.

The little farm carts are almost swallowed up in the press of the people, but for a second we can see the heads and shoulders of the condemned moving slowly, very slowly, on their way to the scaffold. As they pass out of sight our ears catch the beginnings of the roaring of the crowds on the corner of the Quai de l'Horloge and the Pont au Change.

V

If we stay too long at the top of the balustrade we are liable to be asked our business by one of the gendarmes at the main entrance to the Law Courts, so we had better go down the steps and see what there is today behind the little courtyard.

The iron gate is always open in the daytime, and we can go down the nine steps and have a drink at a table in the open if the weather is fine. But that doorway, whose story we know, is intriguing, so we open it, and find ourselves in a café with a bar-counter on one side. A number of its normal clientèle of lawyers' clerks, small business men and shopkeepers and a few workmen, are standing or sitting in the room. At a table in the far corner, where it is less well-lit, two women sit arguing with each other in strident voices. High-backed stalls are ranged on one side where lunch is served, and in one of these a cadaverous-looking man is dipping bread into soup with one hand and looking closely into a file of old papers in the other. A large ugly vase holding some flagging flowers stands at the far end of the bar, behind which a man in a white apron and a young woman with a little boy lean on their elbows, talking as they wait for customers.

At the far end of the room is a wall, covered with an indescribable wall-paper and amply decorated with framed advertisements of the numerous apéritifs obtainable at the bar. An old clock on the wall clacks resoundingly, high up near the ceiling. It was this wall which we saw from the other side of the end of the Prisoners' Gallery near the black hole where the condemned women sat on a bench waiting for eternity. So this is it—where these ordinary folk today suck their bread and soup and order their daily drinks, the first and second of the wicket-gates of the Conciergerie clicked the prisoners in and out. Hearts fluttered, breathing was suddenly difficult, and cheeks were wet with tears in this place where the little boy is trying to get a clock-work tank to climb over a telephone directory on top of the bar-counter;

behind that dreary wall-paper and within a few yards of the two argumentative women lies the women's courtyard, with the bell on the wall.

Well, we live today and not yesterday, so we can order our coffee or apéritif without breach of faith, and as we drink we may ponder on the unsentimental French who find nothing wrong in putting an old place which saw such sharp sadness and housed such aching souls to so modest and homely a use.

One last look and we turn away. As we walk back up the steps outside we look at the railings again. They are old and silent; other men and women have passed through this gateway before us, we mean nothing to it, nor to the thick grey granite blocks which support it on each side. These saw Robespierre pass this way, and Charlotte Corday. Who are we?

A stream of voluble people is coming down the main steps, and the courtyard, the Cour du Mai, is busy with wireless police vans and gendarmes. A big case has just finished in one of the courtrooms above, and we wonder if any of the accused shouted loudly enough to be heard on the other side of the river.

Outside on the pavement the five o'clock crowds beseige the boxes at the bus-stops to tear off the little pieces of paper which give them an order of priority for boarding the buses. These are now coming in a thick procession across the bridge on their noisy way to the Gare Parnasse, Gare de Luxembourg and the Sorbonne. There are never enough seats, and the passengers stand packed inside and on the platforms at the back.

This has always been a street of comings and goings, I thought, as I reached Monsieur Krok, gazing anxiously at the jostling crowds by the bridge. He was relieved, he said, to see me at last. He had been waiting for nearly two hours, and wondered if he had mistaken my orders on the telephone.

"You have had a long day, Monsieur," he said, as he fussed about to make sure that I was comfortable.

"Yes, a long day," I heard myself reply.

And I wondered as we sped along the quay by the Louvre and I looked back over the river to the three black pointed towers of the Conciergerie, how much courage or cowardice would I have shown if I had lived here when the Mousetrap was filled with broken people waiting to die?

Garden of the Chapelle Expiatoire. Graves of Swiss Guards

13. HERE THEY RESTED

La Chapelle Expiatoire

i

Of the thousands of men and women guillotined in Paris during the Revolution, the greatest number died in the Place de la Révolution, and of these, more than a thousand were buried in the little cemetery of the Madeleine, in la ville l'Evêque, barely half a mile away to the north-west. Among them were the King and Queen; Vergniaud, orator of the Girondins; the mad and obscene terrorist Hébert; Madame Roland, the brilliant and romantic Girondin; Charlotte Corday, and Adam Lux, the young German from Mayence, who saw her die and was so bewitched by her beauty and her sacrifice that he deliberately sought and found death on the same guillotine; Philippe called "*Egalité*," cousin of the King, who voted for Louis' death and later followed him to the scaffold; the beautiful Princesse de Lamballe, friend of the Queen, who was murdered during the September massacres and whose head and mutilated body were paraded outside the Temple in front of the windows of the royal apartments; vain, foolish Madame du Barry, mistress of Louis XV; and hundreds more, not least in honour the thousand Swiss guards who perished in the defence of the Tuileries on August 10, 1792, and whose real memorial is the lovely Lion of Lucerne in Switzerland.

The body of Madame Elisabeth, sister of the King, and devoted guardian of his two children (afterwards removed to Les Errancis), lay here also—she who shared with the unhappy Royal Family, first the indignities and then the miseries of their life in the Temple. It was to this noble woman that Marie-Antoinette addressed her last letter from the Conciergerie prison on the morning of her execution. It never reached her, and she too died on the guillotine. (What happened to the letter we shall presently see.)

In 1792 this lonely place was set amid cornfields and grass meadows, with the rue d'Anjou on one side and the rue de l'Arcade on the other. Few people lived near, and that is no doubt why the daily load of corpses from the Place de la Révolution was taken here. When the victims were numerous and the grave diggers too few to bury them currently, the bodies lay for a day or more before they were interred. This was the fate of Marie-Antoinette, though nine months earlier Louis XVI had been buried with decency and respect, and a sworn report was made by the priests who conducted the burial.

A certain Monsieur Desclozeaux, a Royalist, lived in one of the few houses in the rue d'Anjou, and this brave man and his son-in-law made exact notes of where in the cemetery the King and Queen had been buried. When with Robespierre's death in July 1794 the Terror came to an end, Monsieur Désclozeaux bought the plot in which the cemetery of la ville l'Evêque stood. On the site of the royal graves he planted some weeping willows, and in their shade the bodies of the King and Queen rested for twenty-two years.

ii

The Allies were peace-making in Vienna, Napoleon was fretting in Elba, and Louis XVIII, fat and gouty brother of the dead Louis, was back in the Tuileries. To him came M. Désclozeaux with his precious news, and the King ordered that a most careful search should be made on the sites indicated. For two days, January 18 and 19, 1815, under official supervision, they dug the ground of the old cemetery; on the first they found the grave of the Queen, and on the second that of the King, close by, exactly where M. Desclozeaux had said they would be.

With what emotion were the bones and few remaining garments (among them the Queen's garters) gathered together and placed in lead coffins, sealed with the royal insignia, and guarded night and day! Then, on January 21, the twenty-second anniversary of Louis XVI's death, the coffins in a long procession passed through the silent, crowded streets of Paris on their last journey to the Bourbon vaults at St. Denis, by the same route the King had travelled to the guillotine. There they rest to-day with their ancestors—those, at least, whose coffins were not desecrated during the Revolution.

On the site of the cemetery of the Madeleine the new King ordered a chapel to be built in their memory, "in expiation of the crime by which they had died." He did not live to see it, and the third brother, Charles X, was King in his turn when the building was finished.

In the crypt of the chapel, on the exact spot where the bones of the King and Queen were found, the mixture of earth and quick lime which had clung to them was placed in a marble sarcophagus, and you may stand in front of it today and ponder on the melancholy story of the well-meaning Louis XVI and the wayward Marie-Antoinette, who suffered so much because of all that had happened in the long history of France before them.

iii

You have probably bought flowers from the stalls by the side of the Madeleine and thought no more about it. You may have walked and shopped, dined and danced, in the rue Royale, and crossed the square behind the great church on the way back to your hotel, with the stars overhead and a gentle breeze stirring the trees in the Boulevard Malesherbes close by. Did you know that all the time you were within five hundred yards of this strange chapel which marks the place where the Revolution buried so many of its dead?

Today the rue d'Anjou, the rue de la Ville de l'Evéque, the rue de l'Arcade, and rue des Mathurins, which bound or lead to the Chapelle Expiatoire, are just off the busy stream, though if you walk down the Boulevard Haussmann at this point you will see the trees of the chapel garden on the left-hand side, where they enclose a kind of square.

There is nothing beautiful about the chapel from the street—it is clumsy and fussy until you push open one of the little gates and walk up the steps to the doors leading to the inner garden which is the cemetery. Then a new beauty spreads itself. The noise of Paris is stilled; here the solid vaults of the Swiss Soldiers stand on guard, and on each side of the gravel path which leads to the chapel are two long common graves, now set with rose trees and ivy-beds enclosing a length of turf, carefully tended.

Manon Phlipon (Madame Roland) lies here, she whose laughter and courage during the long imprisonment before they killed her in October 1793 (the month the Queen died) brightened the lives of her fellow prisoners, who had none of her high intellect and generous spirit and drew from her the strength to die with hope and courage.

Now look up to that block of stone on the right-hand side of the chapel, and stand quietly by the tomb of Charlotte Corday, whose journey to kill a Monster we have followed, and who passed to her own death serene and unafraid.

Walk slowly past the tombs of the Swiss, who fell before Louis' futile order came to them to "lay down their arms." The bones of more than a thousand of them are here, a bare mile from their last battlefield in the gardens, on the steps, and in the halls of the Royal Palace. Perhaps they stirred again in 1871, when the flames of civil strife licked along the Tuileries once more, and devoured at last the buildings they had died defending.

And having noted all these things, go up the steps and into the chapel. You will find yourself in a small but noble place, where no sound enters but the soft echo of your own footfall. Look up to the central dome of the high roof, to the smaller domes which match it, and then down to the lovely statues of the King and Queen on either side.

On the right, Louis, kneeling, is pointed to the skies by an angel, symbol of the Abbé Edgeworth who was with him at the scaffold; the group, carved out of one piece of marble, is the only statue of the King in Paris. On the base, in letters of gold, is the text of Louis' will and testament, written in the Temple and dated on the day of his death. Whatever his faults, calm courage and nobility of mind were not denied him to the end.

"Tell my son never to seek to avenge my death," he wrote. "Teach him, should he unhappily come to be King, to think only of his fellow citizens." Poor little Dauphin! At least his father did not live to see him slowly murdered by ruffians because he was the King's son. (So long as a male Capet lived they feared for the Revolution.)

Of his wife, Louis asked forgiveness for all the unhappiness which he had brought her, begging her to believe he had no fault to find in her. He forgave all those who "with false zeal have striven to do me evil," adding: "In moments of trouble and emotion, we are not always our own masters." Many a greater man than Louis XVI has died without expressing Christian charity in such simple words.

Equally moving is the statue of the Queen. Her proud face gazes steadfastly on the Cross, and at her feet the crown is lost among the folds of her dress. Beneath her statue, to match the other, are the words of her last letter.

As you read the lines, set in gold in two broad columns, you may wonder at the brutality of an age that could deliberately prevent it from reaching the woman who had charge of her children. Marie-Antoinette had her own doubts, for she wrote: "If this should ever reach you."

The day she died the letter was handed to the Public Prosecutor, Fouquier-Tinville. You can read that tiger's last letter, and think how strange it is that a man who could write tenderly to his own wife and children, and who was so good a father, was not melted by the last letter of the Queen as he held it in his hand on October 16, 1793. Frightened, he passed it on to Robespierre, his master, and the cold heart of the man in the Maison Duplay would not let him send it to the King's sister. Instead, he hid it under his mattress, and there it stayed until he himself went down on the hard plank of the guillotine. Did the sad words never burn him as he slept upon them night after night in his little room in the rue St. Honoré?

When the police and officials of the Committee of Public Safety came to collect his effects after his death the letter was found by a member of the Convention, Courtois. By then Madame Elisabeth had followed the King and Queen to the guillotine, and Courtois kept the letter, saying nothing to the others who were in the house with him. Twenty years later, when all were Royalists once more, he wrote from his house in the country to the new King telling him of the letter, of some clothes, and a lock of the Queen's hair, offering them to Louis XVIII in exchange for a pardon for his revolutionary activities. He was arrested, and after the precious relics had been found he was banished to Belgium, and so passes despicably from history.

By the King's command they showed the letter to Marie-Antoinette's daughter, the Duchesse d'Angoulême, the only survivor of the Temple, and when her eyes fell on her mother's handwriting she fainted.

Today the letter is in the Archives, and one may doubt if in all the long story of love, cruelty, baseness and nobility of the human race, anything more moving exists than this piece of yellow paper, closely covered with the lines written by a Queen about to die, stained with her tears, and handed on from one mean man to another until her daughter, now grown to womanhood, held it at last within her trembling fingers.

iv

Turn now to the left and go down the stairs to the crypt, where in a small vaulted and tiled chamber you come to the grey marble tomb which stands on the exact site of the first hurried graves, beneath a round window of coloured glass.

The weeping willows of Monsieur Désclozeaux stood here, and when the wind blew across the fields towards the Place de la Révolution they sheltered the cold burial ground with their long tresses. When it rained they shed their soft tears, so that the grass was always fresh on the earth above the dead King and Queen. The place was quiet; and is, still.

V

Where were Danton, Camille and Lucille Desmoulins, and their friends buried? And Robespierre, St. Just, and those who followed them in July of the same year? If you ask the caretaker at the Chapelle Expiatoire for the leaflet concerning that place when it was the Madeleine Cemetery, you will find their names among those whose bones are still there. In fact, this information is incorrect.

Early in 1794 the Cemetery became overcrowded, and complaints about its condition were so numerous that the authorities decided to close it. This was done on March 24, i.e., roughly a fortnight *before* the *Dantonistes* were executed. The truth is that from that date the bodies of those guillotined in the Place de la Révolution were taken a good mile to the north, to the Errancis Cemetery, near the Parc Monceau. This in its turn was closed three years later, and in 1817 the bones of 1,119 victims of the Terror were transferred, in one confused mass, to the catacombs south of the river (Place Denfert-Rochereau). There they lie today—the guilty with the innocent, the famous with the unknown, in silent and perpetual unrecognition—a state of equality which their owners had certainly not foreseen.

The Errancis Cemetery was at the northern end of the rue du Rocher where it runs into the present Place Prosper-Goubaux. Nothing now remains of this old burial ground. In the middle of the last century these fields became streets and boulevards, part of the new Paris which had nothing to do with the Revolution. Only the records and the researches of devoted men like Lenôtre have fixed the site whch once received such tragic remains.

14. THE WAY OF THE TUMBRILS

i

You will have noticed how often we have had to use our imagination on our pilgrimage of the Revolution through the streets of modern Paris, how whole streets of history, like the old rue des Cordeliers and buildings where great events took place, like the Temple, the Bastille, the Riding School and the hall of the Jacobins Club, have disappeared forever under the housebreakers' picks and axes; or have been so changed, as in the Conciergerie Prison, as to need careful research and scrutiny of maps and plans to establish truly their former outlines.

This business of imaginary reconstruction has, of course, its fascination. There is excitement as first one clue and then another reveals the truth or destroys a myth. If it were not so, if every house and doorway, street and garden, church and graveyard remained untouched by time or the hand of man, guides and guide books would be even duller than they are.

It is fortunate, however, that the route taken by the condemned through Paris at the end of the eighteenth century, that *via dolorosa* which began always at the Conciergerie Prison and in most cases finished in the Place de la Révolution, can be followed today almost in its entirety, over bridges, through streets, and past buildings the majority of which are there today as they were when the passage of the farm carts—the tumbrils—was often a daily sight for more than three tumultuous years.

Today there are only two parts of the route where modern Paris has changed their faces so completely as to require re-identification.

The first is the scene which faces you on the north bank as you cross the Pont Neuf or the Pont au Change from the south. Here—where today the white block of a department store fills the Quai de l'Ecole, with at night its huge lighted "S" leaping amid cascades of golden neon, and on its eastern side the rue de la Monnaie is wide and spacious—here a clutter of old houses and narrow streets stood facing the Seine; and eastwards, along the Quai de la Mégisserie (now the Place du Châtelet, with its monument to many of Napoleon's victories) ran then the little rue St. Germain de l'Auxerrois, hiding behind it a maze of tiny streets and close-built houses which from a historical viewpoint it is a pity to have lost.

Today, on the Quai du Louvre, the shops are full of shirts and shoes, and outside a cinema a crowd is watching an animated window display of a duel in "Fanfan la Tulipe."

The second metamorphosis is along the western half of the rue St. Honoré itself, from the church of St. Roch onwards (where Bonaparte's "whiff of grapeshot" flew) and on the south side especially. Here the street is entirely a new creation, with its modern buildings, smart shops and glimpses of the busy rue de Rivoli from the many short streets leading in that direction. However, on the north side of the rue St. Honoré many of the original houses, some altered and enlarged, survive, and most of the little streets running away to the north are much as they were in the eighteenth century. The famous turn to the left out of the rue St. Honoré into the rue Royale presents today a wider view of the tourists' twentieth century Paris denied to the victims of the Terror as they made that turn and saw before them the guillotine in the Place de la Révolution, and the end of the road.

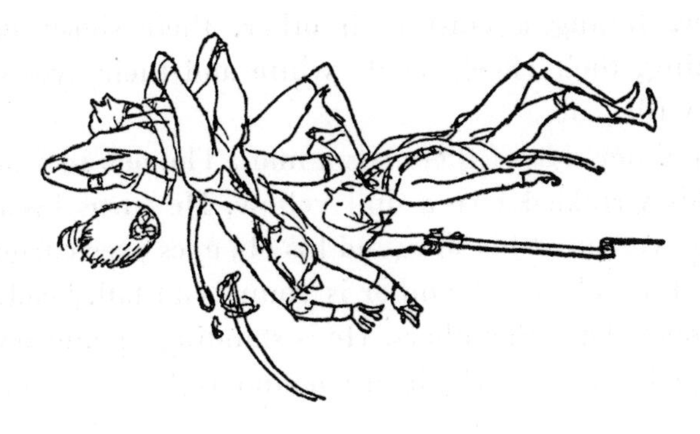

ii

We have seen, in the "Mousetrap" chapter, how the condemned men and women were herded to their places in the tumbrils, and have watched their slow impeded progress across the Cour du Mai, through the iron gateway of the Palais de Justice, and left into the little rue St. Barthelémi (now the wider Boulevard du Palais) which leads to the Seine.

Let us look closely at the occupants of one of these carts on their last journey, along the Way of the Tumbrils. Sanson is in the first cart, looking straight ahead and speaking only occasionally to the driver. He has done this journey so often that the behaviour of the men and women behind him and the noise of the crowds pressing from each side of the streets have ceased to have any effect on him. He is doing the job he is paid for; he has nothing to do with the rights or wrongs of the day's batch, and the sooner the business is over the better pleased he will be.

There are seven condemned in this cart; five men and two women. The women, one young, one old, sit together, falling against each other, their shorn heads touching, their cheeks chalk white and their eyes wide open with fear.

On either side of them sits a man. The one in front is old, his wrinkled face a dull yellow. He turns his back on the woman at his side, and his old eyes peer curiously and calmly ahead; the other is young and tall, head and shoulders above the others. He is standing up and trying to free his hands which are bound tightly behind his back. He calls out frequently to the spectators, telling them they are mad, he is mad, the world is mad, and the end of the world is at hand. The crowds laugh at this and shout back at him: "Your world, citizen, yes, your world is ending!"

Opposite these four sit the other three men; the first is a priest, middle-aged, his eyes shut, lips moving continually in prayer; he is oblivious of the crowds and of his companions. The man next to him is much older, perhaps seventy. He is shorter than the other two, and shows signs of great agitation. He jerks his grey head—a fine, distinguished head with noble features—this way and that, his mouth opens and shuts, shuts and opens, opens and shuts again, and no sound emerges. His eyes are half closed, and from them the tears run down his cheeks to his open neck. On his right, near the back of the cart, is a young man who sits boldly upright; his large head, with masses of dark brown hair (except at the back, where it is shorn from the nape of his neck upwards) seems to be asking the world a question, to which his dark eyes find no answer. Every now and then he turns towards the old man by his side and speaks a few words of encouragement and comfort in a deep, cultured voice. The old man is turning eagerly, pathetically, towards him, and now he leans over so that his drooping shoulder touches the broad chest of his young companion; he stays like that for a long time.

Now at last he feels a strange lightness; suddenly his dreadful fears of the last day and night have gone; he longs for the end to come. Although he can see that the streets on either side of the cart are filled with people, he does not look at them; he looks up either at the sky, which is getting dark in the east, or down at his feet braced against the wooden floor of the cart. His eyes are still full of tears, and he cannot wipe them dry, because his hands are tied behind his back. There is a roaring in his ears like the sound of the sea on the shore when he was a child. He is not sure whether this noise is something going on inside his head, or coming in from outside, but he notices that it is louder at one moment than at the next.

As they pass the great blue and gold clock on the corner of the Quai de l'Horloge, the roaring noise is very loud. The crowds are thick at this point by the river bank. Then he knows that the noise in his ears is coming from the people in the street. He wonders if they know that he is there by mistake? (They had not even called his name properly when Fouquier-Tinville shouted at him in the court-room.)

And now he feels a great anxiety to know which route Sanson will take across the river. He prays that they may go over the Pont au Change, because then they will leave the Conciergerie behind them. But if Sanson orders the driver to turn to the left along the quay they will pass that dreadful place along its whole length, and he cannot face that.

He stands up to see better, and in a moment he is down on the floor of the cart, the left side of his face aflame where he has been hit with something unmentionable thrown from the street. He cannot restrain his tears. Again there comes the deep cool voice in his ears.

"Come, my friend. Be brave again, and calm. Let us

help each other. Come, my dear sir. You are older than I—lean again on me."

The old man pushes himself up from the floor on to the bench again. He had barely noticed the other men and women in the cart when they were thrown into it from the steps of the Conciergerie, and now he looks up closely at the young man who is talking to him. He gazes at the strong, sensitive face and deep-set dark eyes.

He thinks: "I must try to thank him. I must be as brave as I can." But no words come from him at all. It does not matter, words are not needed, they are smiling at each other.

Now they are almost across the bridge; he can feel the cool air from the river on his face. It is wonderful after the heavy stench of the street filled with people. The others in the cart are looking to the left, to the west, and his eyes follow theirs.

The sky is ablaze with the colours of the setting sun, and on either bank ahead he sees the outlines of buildings he has known all his life, the dome of the Four Nations on the left bank, and the dark mass of the Louvre on the right; beyond it the trees of the Tuileries gardens line the river, and just beyond . . . "It is as close as that," he thinks, suddenly.

A great press of people awaits them on the Quai de la Mégisserie, and as the cart turns to the left, leaving the Pont au Change behind, he can see now that they are shouting and shaking their fists and throwing things at one of the carts behind. In the second cart, a man jumps to his feet and starts to sing. In a moment they are all singing, and as the sound of their voices reaches him he can hear that they are singing the Marseillaise. It is not his song, he has never sung it; but something irresistible seizes them all, and in the first cart they too stand and sing the song of the Revolution.

Now the old man can feel the cart jolting heavily over the roughness of the Quai de la Mégisserie. On the far side of the Seine the sun touches the three black towers of the Conciergerie—César, d'Argent, Bonbec—and he is filled with elation, with a sense of escape, the prison is now so far away. "It is we who will live," he hears himself shouting.

They have come to the Pont Neuf, and he can see more people pressed against the parapet, and their gaze is over the old bridge towards the Place Dauphine, to the house of Madame Roland. He thinks of her cry, on the steps of the scaffold: "Oh, Liberty! What crimes are committed in thy name!" And he remembers that with his sister he had attended his first school in the Place Dauphine; it was always very quiet there.

Here they turn right-handed, into the rue de la Monnaie and rue du Roule. These little streets are very dark and narrow, and he is afraid because of the closeness of the people; a man spits at him. They are yelling again now, and for a moment the cart halts. But only for a moment, for Sanson is shouting back at the mob and he has said something which makes them laugh. The cart moves forward again.

At the end of the rue Chaussetterie they turn in a creaking procession, one cart after another, eastwards into the rue St. Honoré. Here the crowds are not so thick, but every window beside and above them, and every balcony, is filled with people. Some are shouting and cursing, some laugh and wave scarves and handkerchiefs, a few just watch, silent. The old man catches the eye of a woman at a window. She is crying, and he calls out to her: "Farewell, friend. Do not cry for us, but for yourselves."

The young man begs him to keep quiet. His foolish cry of "friend" may bring police spies to that house and that window this very night to take the woman away. Robespierre and Fouquier have their spies in every street. The old man is overcome and buries his head in his knees.

Their passage down the long street seems endless. It must be an hour since they started. He thinks: "Why do we go so slowly? Do they not know that we wish to die quickly? That already part of us is dead?"

The priest on the bench opposite is praying aloud in a soft and wandering voice: "Mother of God, pray for us all; pray for me; pray for us all." Over and over again, and the old man says: "Amen, amen," and all the others join in. The driver looks round and barks: "Shut up! You will need more than prayers when Sanson touches the back of your necks." The priest pays no attention. "Mother of God, pray for all of us," "Amen, amen," they answer.

The air is lighter now as they pass the gates of the Palais-Royal. In a dream the old man recalls the walks in the sunshine of these gardens with his children and his dear wife, who has gone on this road before him. Suddenly his throat tightens, and the tears come flooding over his cheeks again. He thinks: "But I shall see her soon, why do I cry?"

Now the shouting in the street has ceased. On their right is the rue du Marché St. Honoré, and down there is the Jacobins Club. The mob are not allowed to congregate here. Soon they pass the Maison Duplay, Robespierre's house. Some of the men in the carts start singing again, raising their voices in defiance as they go by.

And now at last they reach the end of the rue St. Honoré. Already their cart is swinging round into the rue Royale, and one of the drivers points in the direction the cart is taking. They all know what he means, and the old man knows too. Over the heads of Sanson and the driver he sees the wide open space of the Place de la Révolution; there is the guillotine, bleak and black against the sky. How small it looks! He had thought it would fill the whole square.

Now the carts are in the square itself; round the scaffold lines of soldiers face in every direction, a mounted captain is giving orders, he has plumes in his hat of red and white and blue. Hemming in the soldiers is a great mass of people, shouting and singing.

The cart jolts forward a short distance, and stops. Sanson gets down, and in a moment goes up the steps to his assistant waiting on the platform of the guillotine. One by one the men and women in the cart are pulled out over the side. As each in turn goes up the steps to be bound to the plank the crowd is silent; as the knife falls they roar like the sea breaking on great cliffs.

Now it is the old man's turn. He hesitates, is pushed up from behind, and for a second looks out over the thousands of people. In the silence his voice is heard asking the man who holds him if he should bless them now, or after? The man gives him a strange smile, and looks up at the knife.

Only the executioner's assistant at the foot of the scaffold, sweating because there have been so many in the carts, notices on one dead face in the basket a look of unusual serenity.

15. MONSIEUR KROK DRIVES AWAY

On my last day in Paris, a few months ago, I sought out my friend Monsieur Krok, and it was like old times to be sitting back in the ancient car while the maestro juggled it through the busy traffic.

I was staying in the rue de Rivoli, and my high window overlooked the Tuileries gardens. That morning I got up early. It was midwinter, and during the night it had snowed steadily. When I pulled the curtains aside it was barely light and the lamps below were still shining, brightly reflected in the white road and in the snow-laden branches of the trees; in the great courtyard of the Carrousel and around the small triumphal arch of Napoleon they twinkled in the frosty air.

Along the short Avenue Paul Déroulède, connecting the rue de Rivoli with the north bank of the Seine and running in front of the open space where the Palace of Catherine de Médici once stood, the buses passed to and fro, their headlights turning the white snow to pale yellow. I could hear the bark of their diesel engines. A blue and silver motor coach drew up noisily to spill its load of school children on to the pavement where some nuns were waiting for them, the winter wind making strange shapes of their white coifs as they formed the children up into two long rows and marched them off in the direction of the Louvre. From everywhere, down the street and by all the varied pathways across the gardens I could see the black figures of early workers hurrying across the snow.

From my third floor window I surveyed the familiar scene in the heart of modern Paris, and my thoughts began to wander. Over there was the wide Carrousel, across which the Royal Family had escaped that summer night disguised as the Baroness de Korff, her children and a tutor. A few hundred yards to my left, at the corner of a little street long since swallowed up, Fersen the Swede had waited for them with his great *berline*, and from there the journey had begun, to end just short of the frontier at Varennes, where the ferocious postmaster of Ste. Menehould, the zealot Drouet, identified the King and Queen under the wavering glare of peasants' torches.

I thought, too, of the young artillery officer, Bonaparte, hurrying from his lodgings near the Palais-Royal on August 10, 1792 to watch, from a little window overlooking the Carrousel, the onslaught on the Palace by the men and women from the Faubourg St. Antoine. When the fighting stopped he walked into the gardens and after a few minutes turned away in disgust and anger at the terrible things he saw. He never forgot this experience of what mob-rule in the raw could mean, and it was then that in the young Napoleon's mind were born a hatred of anarchy and a vision of dictatorship to come.

Where the nuns had disappeared with their school children, Louis XVI with Marie Antoinette at his side had put the Phrygian cap of liberty, with its tricolour rosette, on the head of the little Dauphin to satisfy the mob; here, later, Napoleon had brought Josephine from an Empress' crowning at Notre Dame; and it was from here, later still, that his nephew Napoleon III had kissed the Empress Eugénie farewell as he set out on his struggle with Bismarck that ended in disaster at Sedan.

Now it was daylight, and the first of the flood of shining motorcars and taxis were beginning to glide towards the Place de la Concorde along the one-way rue de Rivoli. I could hear the shopkeepers in the arcades below taking down their shutters to display in their bright windows the cheap jewellery, smart belts and bags, scent and soap, to tempt the tourists now descending on them. Further along, towards the rue Royale, men on ladders were polishing the plate glass windows which house the silk shirts and dressing gowns from the best houses of Piccadilly and St. James's Street.

I had ordered Monsieur Krok to be at the hotel early, and looking down I could see the black roof of his cabriolet. I packed my bag quickly, swallowed half-cold the coffee the waiter had brought in while I was day-dreaming at the window, paid my bill and in a moment was sitting in the car. Monsieur Krok enveloped my thighs and legs in a huge fur rug.

"Drive me to the very top of Montmartre, Monsieur Krok, if you please," I said.

Away we went, through the rapidly filling streets until we turned away up the hill and through the little streets which most tourists persist in seeing only at night —the streets which Utrillo has fixed with such magic into immortality. Above us now, and getting closer, were the domes of the Sacré Coeur, pink and white as the morning sun caught the snow on their curving beauty. At the summit we stopped, and disengaging myself with some difficulty from the fur rug I got out and looked back over the city in which for all these years I had been looking for ghosts and listening for echoes.

If you have never looked at Paris from here, with the rising sun touching the Seine and its bridges and the church towers and steeples, and the domes and arched roofs of the great buildings, and black and beautiful far away the mass on the Ile de la Cité which is Notre Dame, you have not seen Paris.

I fixed my glasses on the Eiffel Tower, and thought of Robespierre and his great feast on the Champ de Mars nearby; swept my view east along the river to the Invalides, and for the thousandth time wondered if Napoleon, now a tiny thing lying there encased in his many lead coffins and his shining mausoleum, was a long way before, or after, his time; rested the glasses on the sprawling mass of the Louvre, its roofs now glittering in the shafts of sunlight, and felt, from this high distance, the power and majesty of the great King who gave it shape; searched for and thought I could pick out, south of the river, the Luxembourg in its gardens, and remembered for a moment Danton's last night of freedom in the little streets this side of it; swung my view in a great arc to where the Bastille had stood, and further north, though I could not pinpoint it, in the confused mass of roofs and churches, the Square du Temple, and tried to visualise the grim Tower as it must have looked when Louis and Marie-Antoinette lived their last languishing days inside its massive walls.

And now I turned full to the north, in the direction of St. Denis. I could not see it, but there, as I stood on the hill of Montmartre that morning, I knew that their tormented remains rested at last with their ancestors.

Back in the car and with the fur rug to warm me I sat bemused as the familiar sights and sounds sailed by. I called to Monsieur Krok to drive me for an hour or so along the streets and boulevards we had visited so often together; down the rue de Rivoli, in front of the site of the Tuileries Palace, over the Pont Neuf and into the little streets of Marat and Danton (we stopped for a minute to take a photo of the statue of the Tribune of the People), then across the Place Dauphine to look once again at the great gates of the Palais de Justice; and so back over the river to the Louvre and all the way down the rue St. Honoré into the rue Royale; and finally with a grand sweep and much blowing of his old horn right round the Place de la Concorde until, at my signal, he drew up by the gates of the Tuileries gardens, close by the place where Marie-Antoinette died.

"Well, my friend," I said when he had switched off his motor, "it is done. My searches are over, and my chapters are written."

Monsieur Krok got out and took off his cap with its flat shiny peak. His face was criss-crossed with smiles, and his eyes were bright.

"It is for me to thank you, monsieur," he said with animation. "Because of you, my dear sir, I have learned a new Paris—the old Paris" (he laughed at his little joke). "I have thought about these people, these Kings and Queens and orators whom you have been trying to find, and I often speak about all this in our little café in the evenings. My friends are quite amazed. They ask me if this is all true, and I tell them: "Yes, it is all true. I have been there with my Englishman!"

Then he climbed back into the driver's seat which was like a greenhouse, started the great engine, twiddled the levers on the high steering column as he always did, and sailed majestically away, bowing and waving. I watched him turn in front of the Crillon, and the last I saw of the high old carriage it was accelerating past Marly's horses into the Champs Elysées.

And now I stood for a few minutes, thoughts tumbling through my brain in a cascade. The buses, cars and cycles speed and turn in the vast roundabout of the *Place*, circling the obelisk which stands where the knife of the guillotine rose and fell. The pedestrians crowd together on the pavements at the end of the rue Royale, waiting impatiently for the lights to change from red to green where those in the carts came face to face with their life's end. The evening rush into the subways of the Métro is in full spate. Here, between the Tuileries gardens, the National Assembly, the Madeleine, and the entrance to the Champs Elysées is the centre of Paris, the living heart of France. *Place de la Concorde!*

In this, the most noble square in the world, every kind of drama, pageant, commotion and riot for centuries has filled its moment of destiny. If it is true that every sound since the beginning of time echoes still in the pregnant air around us, then Louis' last call to Frenchmen, drowned by the drums, the song of the Marseillaise pouring from the throats of the dying Girondins, Charlotte Corday's simple request to Sanson, the roaring of the people as the knife fell on Marie-Antoinette and Robespierre, and the great voice of Danton giving his last command to the executioner—all these vibrate still in this vast place amid the discordant uproar of a later age, which, like theirs, has suffered much for freedom.

INDEX

INDEX

M

N

Q

R

S

T

Signing the Rights of Man in the Tennis Court at Versailles

The royal family leaving Versailles

Before storming the Bastille outside the Palais Royal

Early scenes from the French Revolution